Clockwise from top left: Beale Street Landing; statue of Elvis on Beale Street by Andrea Lugar; Sun Studio; Downtown Memphis from Mud Island River Park.

Memphis

MEMPHIS

MARGARET LITTMAN

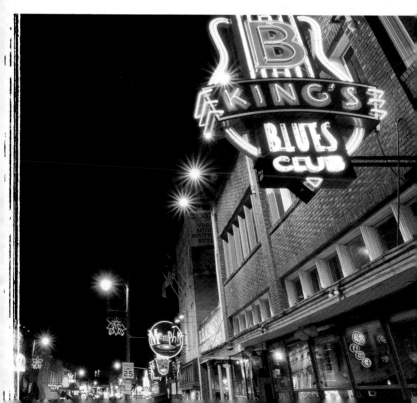

Contents

Take away music and Memphis would lose its soul. Memphis may owe its existence to the mighty Mississippi, but it is music that has defined this Southern metropolis. Memphis music started with the spirituals and work songs of poor Mississippi Delta cotton farmers who came to Memphis and created a new sound: the Memphis blues. The blues then spawned its own offspring: soul, R&B, country, and, of course, rock 'n' roll as sung by a poor truck driver from Tupelo, Mississippi, named Elvis Presley.

On any given night you can find joints where the music flows as freely as the booze, and sitting still is not an option. On Beale Street, music wafts from inside smoky bars out onto the street, inviting you to come inside for a spell. And on Sundays, the sounds of old-fashioned

---

Clockwise from top left: the popular B. B. King's Blues Club; the Blues Hall of Fame; duck march at the famous Peabody Hotel Memphis; Gibson Guitar Factory; A trip to Memphis wouldn't be complete without Rendezvous barbecue.

spirituals and new gospel music can be heard at churches throughout the city.

Memphis music is the backbeat of any visit to the city, but it by no means is the only reason to come. For as rich and complicated as Memphis's history is, this is a city that does not live in its past. Since the 1990s, Memphis has gone through a rebirth, giving new life to the region as a tourist destination. An NBA franchise (the Grizzlies) arrived, the National Civil Rights Museum opened on the grounds of the historic Lorraine Motel, a fantastic AAA baseball field opened downtown, and Memphis made its mark with films such as *Hustle & Flow, Forty Shades of Blue,* and *Black Snake Moan.*

While you're here, you can sustain yourself on the city's world-famous barbecue, its fried chicken and catfish, and its homemade plate lunches, not to mention nouveau Southern eats. Eating may not be why you come, but it might be why you stay. Memphians are gregarious and proud of their city. Don't be surprised if someone invites you over for a Sunday fried chicken supper.

Clockwise from top left: Young Avenue Deli; the Memphis Redbirds play at Autozone Park; exhibit at the Blues Hall of Fame; the Memphis Rock 'n' Soul Museum.

Planning Your Trip

Where to Go

You can knock out Memphis's main attractions in a weekend, but it takes a bit longer to soak up the city's special mojo: the music, food, and laid-back attitude. In fact, if you want more than just a taste of Memphis's famous blues, its legendary barbecue, or its rich history, plan to stay at least a week.

Choose downtown Memphis as your home base. The city center is home to the best bars, restaurants, sports venues, live-music clubs, and, of course, Beale Street. Downtown is also the liveliest, and one of the safest, parts of Memphis after the sun sets.

While a lot of Memphis's attractions are downtown, others are located in the eastern and southern stretches of the city. A free shuttle is available to Graceland and Sun Studio from downtown, but for other attractions like the Stax Museum of American Soul Music and the Memphis Brooks Museum of Art, you will need a car or taxi. Take note that two of the city's best barbecue joints (a Memphis must), as well as its most famous juke joints, are not within walking distance of downtown.

When to Go

Memphis is a city with four seasons. The average temperature in January is 41°F, and in July it hits 81°F. Summer is certainly the most popular season for visiting—Elvis Week in August sees the most visitors of all—but the hot, humid Memphis summer is not for the faint of heart. Even in the South, where people are used to hot and humid, the Memphis humidity can be oppressive.

The best time to visit Memphis is May, when summer is still fresh and mild, and the city puts on its annual Memphis in May celebration. Memphis

Feasting on Rendezvous barbecue is part of the Memphis experience.

Graceland during the holidays

in May includes the World Championship Barbeque Cooking Contest, the Beale Street Music Festival, and the Memphis International Festival.

Fall is also a good choice. The Memphis Music and Heritage Festival held over Labor Day weekend is a great reason to come to Memphis, and probably the best choice for fans of traditional Memphis music.

But if you can't come when the weather is temperate, don't fret. Memphis attractions are open year-round, and the city continues to rock, day in and day out.

Transportation

Visitors making a getaway to Memphis should be able to subsist on public transportation, ride-hailing companies, and taxis. Memphis also has Ride the Roo, a sleek black mini-bus (which serves alcohol) that makes 12 stops along nightlife-heavy areas in Overton Square and Cooper-Young.

If you are flying in, Memphis has international airports, which generally have the best airfare deals.

What to Pack

A cell phone with a good roaming plan and Wi-Fi should cover your basic needs, but a calling card that will work at pay phones and hotels, particularly if you are likely to get off the interstate and out of the range of cell phone signals, isn't a bad idea.

Since your trip could include a fair amount of driving, download a mess of tunes. Depending on your destination, pick up some classic country, bluegrass, blues, or Elvis albums to get you in the mood.

Cowboy boots and a cowboy hat aren't required, but they're certainly always appropriate. Grab some stylin' sunglasses for all the photos you'll take.

Brews in Bluff City

Memphians love their beer, and, lucky for them, there's never been a shortage of places to pop a cold one. Check out a few of these local microbreweries:

The **Memphis Made Brewing Co.,** (768 S. Cooper St., 901-207-5343, memphismadebrewing. com, Fri. 4pm-9pm, Sat. 1pm-9pm, Sun. 1pm-6pm) has some serious beer cred. Head brewer /co-founder Drew Barton was former head brewer at French Broad Brewery in North Carolina. Co-founder Andy Ashby also co-founded the Cooper-Young Beerfest. The brewery puts out one year-round brew (plus a handful of seasonals). There's no food on the menu, but local food trucks often stop by.

Take a tour of **High Cotton Brewing Co.,** (598 Monroe Ave. 901-543-4444, Thurs 4pm-8pm, Fri. 4pm-9pm, Sat. 2pm-10pm, Sun. noon-6 pm) on Saturdays at 3pm. The cost is $12 and includes a pint glass and samples. Or come by for a drink and live music throughout the week.

Tours and brews that have been given nods from national magazines like Men's Journal's list of 100 best beers or available at **Wiseacre Brewing Co.** (2783 Broad Ave., 901/888-7000, wiseacrebrew.com, Thurs. 4pm-8pm, Fri. 4pm-10pm, Sat. 1pm-8pm). The brewery was founded by brothers Kellan and Davin Bartosch; "Wisacre" comes from the name their grandmother used to call them.

The Best of Memphis

Day 1

Arrive in Memphis and check into a downtown hotel, such as the Peabody or Big Cypress Lodge. Grab some Gus's World Famous Fried Chicken and stroll down to Beale Street in the evening. Hear live music at jazz clubs like King's Palace and B. B. King's.

Day 2

Take the Beale Street Walking Tour in the morning, stopping at the W. C. Handy Home and Museum. Take your picture with the Elvis statue, and go treasure hunting at A. Schwab. Eat lunch at the Little Tea Shop downtown, and then head over to Mud Island for the afternoon. Explore the Mississippi River Museum and the River Walk. Eat dinner at The Majestic Grille.

Day 3

Go to the National Civil Rights Museum in the morning, eat lunch along South Main, and then go to the Stax Museum of American Soul Music

Above: Beale Street. **Below:** Stax Museum of American Soul Music.

Photo Ops

There are three things you'll see most often in social media photos of Memphis. One is the **Pyramid.** The other two are a little more artsy.

Artists across town have created **"I Love Memphis" murals,** which also make great photo backdrops. Here are some to check out:

· Cooper and York streets and 645 Marshall Ave. (both by Brandon Marshall)

· 1607 Madison Ave. (by Jean Marie Burks)

· on the greenline near Waring and Minden roads (by Siphne Sylve)

· across the street from the Stax Museum at 926 E. McLemore Ave. (by Whitney Kerr and Jeanynne Lewis, with the help of local artists and students)

· Scott Street and Broad Avenue near Wiseacre Brewing (by Michael Roy)

Another option is the **Amurica Photobooth** (amurica.com), a 1959 teardrop camper decked and transformed into a photo booth. Rent it for an event or pose when you see it at a festival.

and the Blues Hall of Fame that afternoon. After soaking up music history, head to East Memphis for fine dining at Erling Jensen, The Restaurant.

Day 4

Make it Elvis Day. Start early at Graceland to avoid the crowds, and pay your respects over his grave in the Mediation Garden. Then visit Sun Studio, where Elvis recorded his first hit, and where music legends like Jerry Lee Lewis and Johnny Cash also laid down tracks. Eat a burger at Dyer's on Beale Street in memory of the King.

Day 5

Start out at Elmwood Cemetery with the audio tour, and then drive east. Visit the Memphis Brooks Museum of Art and lounge in Overton Park. Check out Levitt Shell for one of their free concerts (pack a picnic!) or tour The Dixon and eat dinner at the Soul Fish in Cooper-Young.

Memphis

Highlights

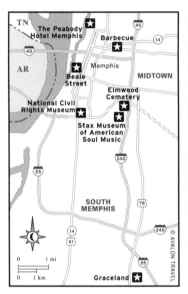

represented the tragic assassination of Martin Luther King, Jr. Today, it tells the story of the African American struggle for civil rights, from before the Civil War to the present day (page 22).

★ **The Peabody Hotel Memphis:** Even the ducks in the fountain get the red-carpet treatment at this landmark hotel. The lobby is a must-visit (page 24).

★ **Stax Museum of American Soul Music:** Irresistible soul music is what made Stax famous in the 1960s, and it is what makes the Stax Museum sweet today. Exhibits bring to life the work of Otis Redding, the Staple Singers, Isaac Hayes, and more (page 32).

★ **Graceland:** The Elvis phenomenon is alive and well. Presley's south Memphis mansion is a testament not only to the King's music, but also his fans (page 33).

★ **Elmwood Cemetery:** Perhaps the most surprising attraction in Memphis, this is the final resting place of dozens of local characters: madams, blues singers, mayors, and pioneers of all types (page 34).

★ **Beale Street:** The street that gave birth to the Memphis blues celebrates its legacy every single night of the week (page 17).

★ **National Civil Rights Museum:** For years the Lorraine Motel merely

★ **Barbecue:** Tangy, juicy, and just a little sweet, Memphis barbecue is the stuff of West Tennessee dreams (page 67).

Memphis is perched atop a low bluff overlooking the majestic Mississippi River (hence one of its official nicknames, Bluff City).

The center city district lies, roughly speaking, along the river. Main Street, a pedestrian-only mall (except for the trolleys) runs north-south, while Union, Madison, and Poplar Avenues are the main east-west thoroughfares. While not compact, central Memphis is entirely walkable for people willing to use a little shoe leather. The Main Street Trolley makes it easy to see downtown and uptown attractions without a car.

In this guide, locations south of Union Avenue are considered downtown, while locations north of Union are uptown. Downtown's main attraction is Beale Street. Also contained within the downtown district is the area known as South Main, a three-block strip along southern Main Street that is home to trendy boutiques, art galleries, restaurants, and condos. South Main is about a 15-minute walk or a 5-minute trolley ride from Beale Street.

Another unique neighborhood in the city center is the Pinch District, located along North Main Street past the I-40 overpass. Originally settled by German immigrants, the Pinch is now a hub of restaurants and nightlife. It is also the gateway to gentrifying residential neighborhoods farther north.

Restaurants in the Pinch have been categorized as uptown in this guide. You can walk to the Pinch, but the best way to get there is to ride the Main Street Trolley.

In 1989, developers created Harbor Town, a New Urban community on Mud Island. The concept was to create a city community that offered amenities such as schools, gyms, entertainment, and restaurants within walking distance of each other. It was also designed to promote a sense of community; homes were built close together with low fences, front porches,

Previous: downtown Memphis; Beale Street.

Memphis

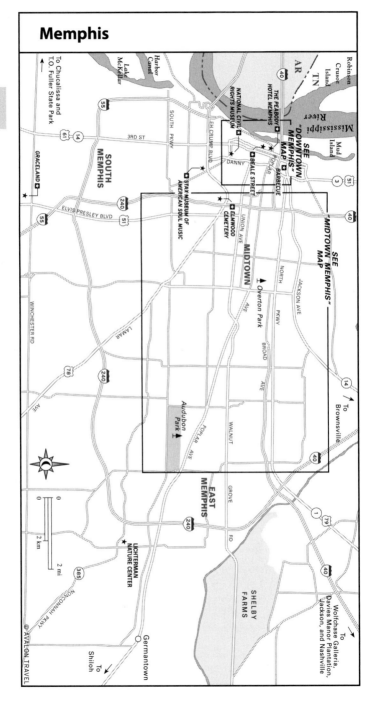

and small yards so that residents would use community parks and green spaces.

In 2007, a boutique hotel opened in Harbor Town, putting the area on the accommodations map for the first time. A major draw for Harbor Town is that it is located right across the river from downtown Memphis but feels like a tight-knit residential community.

Memphis sprawls south, east, and north from the river. Head east from downtown, and you are in midtown, a district of strip malls, aging suburbs, and the city's best park and art museum. Poplar Avenue is the main artery of midtown, and it's a good point of reference when exploring by car (which is really the only way to get around midtown). The city's original suburb, midtown now seems positively urban compared to the sprawling burbs that creep farther eastward every year.

Located within midtown is Cooper-Young, a redeveloping residential and commercial neighborhood that lies around the intersection of Cooper Street and Young Avenue. Since the 1970s, residents of this neighborhood have fought the tide of urban decay by encouraging investment, good schools, and amenities like parks, art galleries, and independent restaurants, and generally fostering a sense of pride in the area. The result is a neighborhood where you'll find lots of restaurants, a great used-book store, record shops, and other attractions that draw the city's young and young at heart.

East Memphis is where you will find large shopping malls, major hospitals, the University of Memphis, and lots of traffic jams. There are also a few attractions out here, the Dixon and the Memphis Botanic Gardens among them.

Generally speaking, north and south Memphis are the most economically depressed areas of the city. Visitors beat a path to attractions like Graceland and Stax in southern Memphis during the day but tend to avoid those areas at night, at least unless they are with a local who knows the way around.

Sights

DOWNTOWN

Downtown refers to the area south of Union Avenue in the city center. It is the heart of Memphis's tourist district.

★ Beale Street

If you want to delve into the history and character of Memphis music, your starting point should be **Beale Street,** home of the blues.

A combination of forces led Beale Street to its place in musical history and popular culture. Named in the 1840s after a war hero, Beale Street was originally part of South Memphis, a separate city that rivaled Memphis during the 1840s.

Downtown Memphis

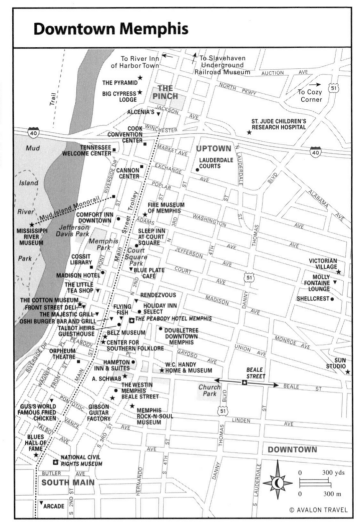

Beginning in the 1850s, and continuing in greater numbers during and after the Civil War, African Americans began to settle along the western part of Beale Street. By the 1880s and 1890s, a middle class of black professionals began to emerge, and Beale Street became the center of commerce, entertainment, and life for many of them. Together with black-owned businesses on Beale Street were laundries, bars, restaurants, pawn shops, and more operated by immigrants from eastern Europe, Ireland, China, Greece, and Germany.

From the 1880s until the 1960s, Beale Street was the epicenter of African American life, not just for Memphians but also for the entire Mid-South region. It was here that blacks felt free from many of society's restrictions.

Beale Street's decline began in the mid-20th century, and by the 1970s it was a shadow of its former self. Investment during the 1980s and 1990s led to the street's rebirth as a destination for tourists and a source of pride for residents, who could now show off the street that gave birth to the blues.

Today, Beale Street has two distinct personalities. During the day it is a laid-back place for families or adults to stroll, buy souvenirs, and eat. You can also stop at one of several museums and attractions located on the street. At night, Beale Street is a strip of nightclubs and restaurants, a great place to people watch, and the best place in the state, if not the country, to catch live blues seven nights a week.

W. C. Handy Home and Museum

The story of Beale Street cannot be told without mentioning William Christopher Handy, whose Memphis home sits at the corner of Beale Street and 4th Avenue. The building was originally located at 659 Jeanette Street, but it was moved to Beale Street in 1985. Now the **W. C. Handy Home and Museum** (352 Beale St., 901/527-3427, wchandymemphis.org, Tues.-Sat. 10am-5pm summer, Tues.-Sat. 11am-4pm winter, adults $6, children $4) is dedicated to telling the story of Handy's life. It was Handy who famously wrote, in his "Beale Street Blues": "If Beale Street could talk, married men would have to take their beds and walk, except one or two who never drink booze, and the blind man on the corner singing 'Beale Street Blues.' I'd rather be there than anyplace I know."

The Handy museum houses photographs of Handy's family, one of his band uniforms, and memorabilia of the recording company that he founded. You can also hear samples of Handy's music.

A. Schwab

During Beale Street's dark days of the 1970s and 1980s, when the clubs and restaurants closed and the pawn shops opened, one mainstay remained: **A. Schwab** (163 Beale St., 901/523-9782, a-schwab.com, winter: Mon.-Weds. noon-6pm, Thurs. noon-7pm, Fri.-Sat. noon-9pm, Sun. 11am-6pm, may stay open later in the summer depending on crowds). This landmark general store opened in 1876 and was owned and operated by the same family until 2011. Originally the source for household necessities for thousands of Delta residents, A. Schwab remains a treasure trove of goods. Here you will find practical items like underwear, hats, umbrellas, cookware, and tools, as well as novelties like old-fashioned candy, incense, and actual cans of Tennessee whoop-ass. Upstairs is the A. Schwab museum, a hodgepodge of old-time tools, clothes, and memorabilia of the store's 130-plus-year history.

The new owners, who purchased the store from the Schwab family, added a turn-of-the-century-style soda fountain, a private event space, and spruced up this landmark for the next century.

Memphis Rock 'n' Soul Museum

Music fans should plan to spend several hours at the **Memphis Rock 'n'**

Beale Street Walking Tour

Beale Street runs from the Mississippi River to Manassas Street in midtown Memphis, but it is the three blocks between 2nd and 4th Streets that really matter. In its heyday, the Beale Street commercial and entertainment district extended farther east and west, but today, it has been condensed into the half-dozen blocks from Main Street to 4th Street. This walking tour begins at the intersection of Beale and Main Streets, and heads eastward.

Near the corner of Beale and Main Streets is the **Orpheum Theatre** (203 S. Main St., 901/525-3000, www.orpheum-memphis.com). This site has been used for entertainment since 1890, when the Grand Opera House opened there with a production of *Les Huguenots*. Later, the opera house presented vaudeville shows and theater. Fire destroyed it in 1923, but in 1928 it re-opened as the Orpheum, a movie theater and performing arts venue for the likes of Duke Ellington, Cab Calloway, Bob Hope, and Mae West. The Orpheum remains one of the city's premier venues for the performing arts, with Broadway productions, mainstream musical artists, and movies.

A block east of the Orpheum is a statue of Memphis's most famous native son, Elvis Presley. Depicting the King during his early career, the statue sits in **Elvis Presley Plaza.**

A. Schwab (163 Beale St., 901/523-9782, a-schwab.com, winter hours: Mon.-Weds. noon-6pm, Thurs. noon-7pm, Fri.-Sat. noon-9pm, Sun. 11am-6pm, may stay open later in the summer depending on crowds) has served Memphis residents for more than 140 years, although it focuses now on odd, out-of-date, and hard-to-find items rather than traditional general-store necessities. Stop in for a souvenir or to visit the A. Schwab "museum," a collection of old-fashioned household tools and implements.

A few doors down from A. Schwab, at the Irish pub Silky O'Sullivan's, you can see what remains of one of Beale Street's most magnificent old buildings. The facade of what was once the **Gallina Building** is held up by six steel girders. From the 1860s until 1914, this facade kept watch on the business empire of Squire Charles Gallina, who operated a saloon, restaurant, and 20-room hotel, as well as a gambling room.

Beyond 3rd Street is **Handy Park,** named for famous blues composer

Soul Museum (191 Beale St., 901/205-2533, www.memphisrocknsoul. org, 10am-7pm daily, adults $12, children 5-17 $9), located right next to FedEx Forum, off Beale Street. An affiliate of the Smithsonian Institution, this museum tells the story of Memphis music from the Delta blues to *Shaft*. Start with a short video documentary, and then follow the exhibits with your personal audio guide, which includes recordings of dozens of Memphis-influenced artists, from B. B. King to Elvis. Exhibits are dedicated to Memphis radio stations; the influence of the Victrola, Sam Phillips, and Sun Studio; and, of course, all things Elvis, among others. It takes several hours to study all the exhibits in detail and to listen to all (or even most) of the music, so plan accordingly.

There is a free shuttle that runs between the Rock 'n' Soul Museum, Graceland, and Sun Studio. Look for the black van with the Sun label's distinctive yellow sun on the side.

and musician W. C. Handy. Beale Street's Market House was torn down in 1930 to build the park. Since it opened, Handy Park has been a popular place for street musicians, peddlers, concerts, and community events, all of which are presided over by the life-size statue of W. C. Handy.

About midway up the southern side of the next block of Beale Street is the **Daisy Theater** (329 Beale St.), built in 1917 as a movie house. Much of the original interior remains today. The theater is closed to the public but may be rented for private events. Contact the Beale Street Development Corporation (866/406-5986) for information.

Across the street from the Daisy Theater is the **New Daisy Theater** (330 Beale St., 901/525-8981, www.NewDaisy.com), built in 1941 as another movie house. The New Daisy is one of Memphis's prime live-music venues, and it books rock and alternative acts from around the country.

Stately and old, the **First Baptist Beale Street Church** (379 Beale St.) was built between 1868 and 1885 and is home to one of the oldest African American congregations in Memphis. In the 1860s, the congregation started to meet under brush arbors at the present location, and the first temporary structure was erected in 1865. The cornerstone was laid for the present building in 1871. The First Baptist Beale Street Church was an important force in Memphis's African American history. It was here that black Memphians published their first newspapers, the *Memphis Watchman* and the *Memphis Free Speech and Headlight*.

Today, **Church Park** is a humble city park. But in 1899, when Robert Church built Church Park and Auditorium at the eastern end of the Beale Street commercial district, the park was something truly special. Church is said to have been the first black millionaire in the South. He was troubled that there were no public parks expressly for Memphis's African American residents, so in 1899 he opened Church Park and Auditorium on six acres of land along Beale Street. The park was beautifully landscaped and manicured, with bright flowers, tropical trees, and peacocks. The auditorium was a venue for black performers and speakers. Church Park remains a venue for community events, particularly the annual Africa in April event every spring.

Gibson Guitar Factory

Across the street from the Rock 'n' Soul Museum is the **Gibson Guitar Factory** (145 Lt. George Lee Ave., 901/544-7998, ext. 4075, www.gibson. com, tours every hour on the hour 11am-4pm Mon.-Sat., noon-4pm Sun., ages five and up $10, under five not admitted), one of three in the United States. The Memphis plant specializes in the semi-hollow-bodied guitar, and a wide range of models are for sale in Gibson's retail shop. On the hour-long tour of the factory floor you can see guitars being made, from the shaping of the rim and panels to the painting and buffing of the finished product. Tours sell out, so reservations are recommended, particularly during the busier summer months. Most factory workers leave by 3pm and have the weekends off, so plan ahead if you want to see the factory floor in full swing.

W. C. Handy

W. C. Handy was born in a log cabin in Florence, Alabama, in 1873. The son and grandson of African Methodist Episcopal ministers, Handy was exposed to music as a child in his father's church. Handy was also drawn to the music of the black laborers of the area, and when he moved to Memphis in the early 20th century, he recognized the wealth of the blues music he heard in bars, on street corners, and in back alleys around Beale Street.

Handy was a trained musician, so he was able to set down on paper the music that had, up until then, been passed from one musician to another.

In 1909, Handy composed Memphis mayor Ed Crump's campaign song, "Mr. Crump," which he later published as the "Memphis Blues." But he is most famous for his composition "St. Louis Blues," published in 1914. Handy also created the "Yellow Dog Blues," "Joe Turner Blues," and "Beale Street Blues." Known as the Father of the Blues, Handy passed away in 1958.

★ National Civil Rights Museum

If you do nothing else while you are in Memphis, or, frankly, the state of Tennessee, visit the **National Civil Rights Museum** (450 Mulberry St., 901/521-9699, www.civilrightsmuseum.org, 9am-5pm Mon., Wed.-Sat., 1pm-5pm Sun., adults $15, students and seniors $14, children 4-17 $12). Built on the Lorraine Motel site, where Dr. Martin Luther King Jr. was assassinated on April 4, 1968, the museum makes a thorough examination of the American civil rights movement, from slavery to the present day. Exhibits display original letters, audio recordings, photos, and newspaper clippings from events including the Montgomery bus boycott, *Brown v. Board of Education,* Freedom Summer, and the march from Selma to Montgomery. Original and re-created artifacts, such as the bus where Rosa Parks made her stand in 1955 and the cell where Dr. King wrote his famous *Letter from a Birmingham Jail,* help to illustrate the story of civil rights.

When Dr. King visited Memphis in March and then again in April 1968, the Lorraine Motel was one of a handful of downtown hotels that welcomed African Americans. The room (and balcony and parking lot) where he spent his final hours has been carefully re-created, and a narration by those who were with King tells the shocking story of his death. Across Mulberry Street, in the building that was once the boardinghouse from where James Earl Ray is believed to have fired his sniper shot, exhibits probe various theories about the assassination, as well as the worldwide legacy of the civil rights movement.

Visitors to the museum can pay an extra $2 for an audio guide—a worthwhile investment. This is a large museum, and it is overflowing with information, so visitors who want to give the displays their due attention should plan on spending 3-4 hours here. A good way to visit would be to tour the Lorraine Motel exhibits first, take a break for lunch, and then go across the street for the second half of the museum when you are refreshed.

Spending half a day here is a powerful experience, and one that raises many thoughts about civil rights. Expect interesting conversations with your travel companions after coming here. The gift shop offers books and videos for more information on the topic.

Admission is free on Monday after 3pm to Tennessee residents. In June, July, and August the museum stays open until 6pm.

Belz Museum of Asian and Judaic Art

The **Belz Museum of Asian and Judaic Art** (119 S. Main St., 901/523-2787, www.belzmuseum.org, 10am-5:30pm Tues.-Fri., noon-5pm Sat.-Sun., adults $6, seniors $5, children $4), formerly Peabody Place Museum, houses one of the largest collections of artwork from the Q'ing dynasty. Forged from the private collection of Memphis developers Jack and Marilyn Belz, owners of the Peabody Hotel and the now shuttered Peabody Place mall, the museum features some 1,000 objects, including an array of jade, tapestries, paintings, furniture, carvings, and other artifacts. The museum is also home to the largest U.S. collection of work by Israeli artist Daniel Kafri.

The Belz Museum's new Holocaust Memorial Gallery includes portraits and testimonials from Jewish survivors of the Holocaust in the *Living On* exhibit.

Blues Hall of Fame

The **Blues Hall of Fame** (421 Main St., 901/527-2583, www.Blues.org, 10am-5pm Mon.-Sat., 1pm-5pm Sun., adults $10, students $8, children under 12 free) has existed as an entity—a project of the Blues Foundation—since 1980. But the physical building that you can tour and experience didn't open until 2015. The $2.9 million building is across the street from the National Civil Rights Museum at the Lorraine Hotel. It celebrates the music for which Memphis is famous and honors the musicians who make it.

More than 350 people have been inducted into the Blues Hall of Fame; of the 130 performers, 120 of them are African American. At the museum, you can learn about all of the inductees and listen to their contributions to the genre.

UPTOWN

Uptown refers to locations along Union Avenue and points north in the center city district. Here downtown workers are more common than tourists, and tall office buildings rise above the city blocks.

The Cotton Museum

The **Cotton Museum** at the Memphis Cotton Exchange (65 Union Ave., 901/531-7826, www.memphiscottonmuseum.org, 10am-5pm Mon.-Sat., noon-5pm Sun., adults $10, seniors $9, students $9, military $8, children 6-12 $7) is located in the broad rectangular room that once was the nerve center of the Mid-South's cotton trade. The Cotton Exchange was established in 1873, and it was here that buyers and sellers of the South's most important cash crop met, and where fortunes were made and lost. Located just steps away from the Mississippi River, the Exchange was the trading floor of Cotton Row, the area of town that was defined by the cotton industry.

The Cotton Museum is home to exhibits about cotton's history, its uses, and the culture that its cultivation gave rise to in Memphis and the Mississippi Delta. There are several videos you can watch, as well as a live Internet feed of today's cotton exchange—now conducted entirely electronically. The nicest thing about the museum, however, is seeing the chalkboard where the prices of cotton around the world were written by hand. There is also a replica of the Western Union office, where buyers and sellers sent telegrams using an intricate system of abbreviations known only to the cotton trade. The museum expanded in 2010, adding more hands-on exhibits and an educational wing.

★ The Peabody Hotel Memphis

The Peabody Hotel Memphis (149 Union Ave., 901/529-4000, www.peabodymemphis.com) is the city's most famous hotel. Founded in 1869, the Peabody was one of the first grand hotels of the South, a place as well known for its elegant balls and big-band concerts as for the colorful characters who sipped cocktails at its famous lounge. Named in memory of the philanthropist George Peabody, the original hotel was located at the corner of Main and Monroe. It closed in 1923, and a new Peabody opened two years later in its present location on Union Avenue. It remained the place to see and be seen for generations of Memphians and Delta residents. It was historian and journalist David Cohn who famously wrote in 1935 that "the Mississippi Delta begins in the lobby of The Peabody Hotel."

Even if you don't stay here, you must stop by the elegant hotel lobby to see the twice-daily march of the **Peabody ducks** (a trip to Memphis is incomplete without this experience). The ducks live on the roof of the hotel and make the journey—by elevator—to the lobby fountain every morning

Learn about the life and legacy of Martin Luther King, Jr. at the National Civil Rights Museum.

at 11am. At 5pm they march out of the fountain, back onto the elevator, and up to their accommodations on the roof.

The hotel employs a duck master who takes care of the ducks and supervises their daily trip downstairs. Watching the ducks is free, frenzied, and undeniably fun. It is also one of the most popular activities among visitors to Memphis, so be sure to get there early and secure a good vantage point along the red carpet to watch the ducks march.

Mud Island

In Memphis, it is sometimes easy to forget that you are just steps away from the great Mississippi River. A trip to **Mud Island** will cure this misperception once and for all. A narrow band of land in the river, Mud Island is home to the **Mud Island River Park and Museum** (125 N. Front St., 901/576-7241, www.mudisland.com, 10am-5pm Tues.-Sun., Apr.-Oct., adults $10, seniors $9, children $7), which has exhibits about early uses of the river, steam- and paddleboats, floods, and much more.

The park's **Mississippi River Museum** begins with a refresher course on European exploration of this region—de Soto, La Salle, and Marquette and Joliet—followed by information about early settlement. The highlight is being able to explore a replica of an 1870s steamboat. In the Riverfolk Gallery there are wax depictions of Mark Twain, riverboat gambler George Devol, and steamship entertainers. The museum also remembers the numerous river disasters that have taken place along the Mississippi.

Admission to the museum includes the **River Walk** at the Mud Island River Park, a five-block scale model of the entire Mississippi River—from Minnesota to the Gulf of Mexico. Walk along the model to see scale representations of cities along the river's path, and read placards about the river's history. On a hot day, wear your bathing suit so you can swim in the wading pool that is located at the end of the model of the river inside the park.

The River Park is also home to an outdoor amphitheater, which in

The Peabody Hotel Memphis

summer hosts big-name concerts, a snack bar, outdoor tables, and restrooms. You can rent canoes, kayaks, and paddleboats to use in the still waters around the Mud Island harbor. Bike rental is also available. Mud Island is the site of the city's dragon boat races, which benefit the work of the Tennessee Clean Water Network. These fundraising events feature teams from local businesses and community organizations paddling 46-foot-long boats festooned with dragon heads in unison.

Admission to the River Park is free. You can pay $4 round-trip to ride the monorail to Mud Island, or you can walk across the monorail bridge for free (offering a great photo/selfie opportunity). The monorail station is on Front Street at Adams Avenue.

Slavehaven Underground Railroad Museum

The legend of the Burkle Estate, a modest white clapboard house on North 2nd Street, has given rise to the **Slavehaven Underground Railroad Museum** (826 N. 2nd St., 901/527-3427, www.slavehavenundergroundrailroadmuseum.org, 10am-5pm Mon.-Sat. summer, 10am-4pm Mon.-Sat. winter, adults $10, youth $8). The museum here tells the story of slavery and the legendary Underground Railroad, which helped thousands of slaves escape to freedom in the North (and, after the 1850 Fugitive Slave Act, to Canada). Jacob Burkle, a German immigrant and owner of the Memphis stockyard, is said to have built the Burkle Estate around 1850. Escaping slaves would have hidden in a root cellar beneath the house before making the 1,500-foot trip to the banks of the Mississippi, where they made a further journey north.

Skeptics say that there is no evidence of this story and even point to documents that show that Burkle may not have purchased the property until 1871, well after the end of slavery. Advocates for the Underground Railroad story say that it was the nature of the railroad to be secret, so there is nothing unusual about a lack of concrete evidence.

Mud Island River Park is a great place to take in views of downtown and the mighty Mississippi.

The Birth of Mud Island

Mud Island rose from the Mississippi River as a result of two seemingly small events. In 1876, the river shifted slightly about 20 miles south of Memphis, causing the currents that flowed past the city to alter course. And then, in 1910, the U.S. Navy gunboat, the USS *Amphitrite*, anchored at the mouth of the Wolf River for almost two years, causing a further change in silt patterns. When the ship left in 1912, the sandbar continued to grow, and Mud Island was born.

Residents initially disliked the island, since it was ugly and proved to be a danger to river navigation.

Beginning in the 1930s, poor Memphians squatted on Mud Island in ramshackle homes built of scrap metal and wood. Between 200 and 500 people lived on the island during this time.

In 1959, a downtown airport was built on the island, but the airport was closed in 1970 when the DeSoto Bridge was built. In 1974, plans were developed for what is the present-day Mud Island River Park, which includes a full-scale replica of a riverboat, a monorail to the island, and the signature 2,000-foot flowing replica of the Mississippi River.

Visitors today need not be too concerned with the details of the debate; the Slavehaven museum does a good job of highlighting the brutality of the slave trade and slavery and the ingenuity and bravery it took for slaves to escape. Perhaps the most interesting part of the exhibit are the quilts that demonstrate the way that slaves used quilting patterns to send messages to one another. Other displays show advertisements for Memphis slave auctions and images from the early 20th century that depict damaging racial stereotypes.

The museum is operated by Heritage Tours of Memphis, and staff is available to conduct guided tours of the property.

Fire Museum of Memphis

The **Fire Museum of Memphis** (118 Adams Ave., 901/320-5650, www.fire-museum.com, 9am-6pm Mon.-Sat., 1pm-6pm Sun. summer, 9am-4:30pm Mon.-Sat., 1pm- 4:30pm Sun. winter, adults $10, seniors $8, children $8, family pack for four is $30) is a good place to take children. There is a huge display of fire-engine toys, lots of firefighting paraphernalia, and a "fire room" that presents important lessons on fire safety. You can also see old-fashioned fire engines, and youngsters will enjoy playing in the kid-friendly fire truck. The museum is located in the old Fire Station No. 1 in downtown Memphis.

St. Jude Children's Research Hospital

The sprawling complex of **St. Jude Children's Research Hospital** on uptown's northern fringe has been saving lives and bringing hope to children and their families since 1962. St. Jude was founded by entertainer Danny Thomas in fulfillment of his promise to God to give back to those in need. Over the years and thanks to the success of its fundraising arm—the American Lebanese Syrian Associated Charities—St. Jude has expanded many times over and now leads the world in research and treatment of catastrophic childhood diseases, especially pediatric cancers. Programs with country music stars only expand the reach of St. Jude's and its work. The hospital never turns anyone away due to inability to pay, and it never makes families without insurance pay for their treatment.

Call in advance to tour a small museum about Danny Thomas and St. Jude in the **Danny Thomas ALSAC Pavilion** (332 N. Lauderdale St., 901/578-2042, www.stjude.org, 8am-4pm Sun.-Fri., 10am-4pm Sat., except when there are special events, free), located inside a golden dome on the hospital grounds. Just outside are the graves of Danny Thomas and his wife, Rose Marie. Hospital tours available Mon. through Fri. at 10am and 1pm.

The Pyramid

The Memphis **Pyramid** is the most physically dominating feature of the northern city skyline. Memphis's affiliation with all things Egypt began with its name and continued in 1897, when a large-scale replica of a pyramid was built to represent Memphis at the Tennessee Centennial Exhibition in Nashville. Pyramids were popular symbols on Memphis paraphernalia for many years.

The first serious proposal for a life-size pyramid to be built in Memphis was written in the 1970s, but the idea did not take off until the 1980s, when the city and county governments agreed to fund it. Denver developer Sidney Shlenker promoted the plan and promised restaurants, tourist attractions, and lots of revenue for the city. The 321-foot pyramid was built and opened in 1991, minus the money-making engines that Shlenker promised.

For years the $63 million "Great American Pyramid" sat empty. In spring 2015 this changed. Bass Pro Shops at the **Pyramid** (1 Bass Pro Dr., 901/291-8200, www.basspro.com, 8am-10pm Mon.-Sat., 8am-7pm Sun.)

The Pyramid was revitalized by Bass Pro Shops Outdoor World.

opened what it modestly calls "one of the most dynamic, immersive retail stores in the world." This outdoor gear store includes a cypress swamp, 10 aquariums holding 600,000 gallons of water, a Big Cypress Lodge 105-room hotel (800/225-6343, big-cypress.com) with treehouse cabins, a spa, Ducks Unlimited National Waterfowling Heritage Center, Uncle Buck's Fishbowl and Grill nautical-themed restaurant, a giant 28-story freestanding elevator, and more. Obviously, this isn't an average store. There are regular aquarium and fish feedings (10am and 5pm daily) and alligator feedings (2pm Tues., Thurs., and Sat.).

MIDTOWN

You'll need a car to explore the attractions in midtown, which sprawls along Union, Poplar, and Madison Avenues as they head eastward from the city center.

Sun Studio

It is well worth your time to drop by the famous **Sun Studio** (706 Union Ave., 800/441-6249, www.sunstudio.com, 10am-6pm daily, adults, $12, kids 5-11 free, under 5 not admitted), where Elvis Presley recorded his first hit, "That's All Right," and where dozens of blues, rock, and country musicians recorded during the 1950s. Founded by radioman and audio engineer Sam Phillips and his wife, Becky, the studio recorded weddings, funerals, events, and, of course, music. Phillips was interested in the blues, and his first recordings were of yet-unknown artists such as Rufus Thomas and Howlin' Wolf. In 1953, Elvis Presley came into the studio on his lunch break to record a $3 record of himself singing "My Happiness" for his mother. Phillips was not impressed with the performance, and it was not for another year—and thanks to the prodding of Phillips's assistant, Marion Keisker—that Phillips called Presley in to record some more. When Phillips heard Elvis's version of the blues tune "That's All Right," he knew he had a hit. And he did.

But the story of Elvis's discovery is just one of many that took place in the modest homemade Sun Studio, and this attraction is not just for Elvis fans. The one-hour tour of the studio leaves every hour on the half hour, and while you are waiting you can order a real fountain drink from the snack bar or browse the shop's collection of recordings and paraphernalia. The studio is still in business; you can record here for $75 an hour at night, and dozens of top-notch performers have, including Grace Potter, Beck, and Matchbox Twenty.

Tours start every half hour during business hours and take approximately 90 minutes. Children under the age of five are not permitted on the tours. There are free shuttles from Graceland and the Rock 'n' Soul Museum to Sun Studio.

Lauderdale Courts/Uptown Square

Perhaps the least-known Elvis attraction in Memphis is **Lauderdale Courts**

Midtown Memphis

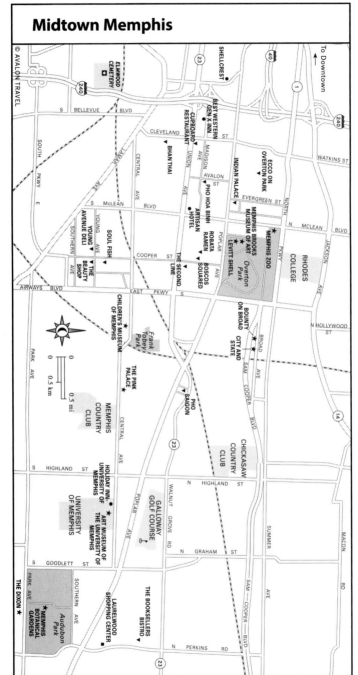

(252 N. Lauderdale St., 901/523-8662, $10 for adults, $7 12 and under, rent the room for the night $250), the public housing complex where Presley lived with his parents from 1949 to 1953, before his rise to fame. The handsome brick building was saved from the wrecking ball in the 1990s thanks to its history with the King, and the apartment where the Presleys lived has been restored to its 1950s glory. Most of the year, the Lauderdale Courts Elvis suite is rented out as a hotel room, but during Elvis's Birthday Week in January and Elvis Week in August it is open for public tours.

Victorian Village

Set on a tree-lined block of Adams Avenue near Orleans Street is Victorian Village, where a half-dozen elegant Victorian-era homes escaped the "urban renewal" fate of other historic Memphis homes.

Visitors can tour the **Woodruff-Fontaine House** (680 Adams Ave., 901/526-1469, www.woodruff-fontaine.com, noon-4pm Wed.-Sun., $10), one of the street's most magnificent buildings. Built in 1870 for the Woodruff family and sold to the Fontaines in the 1880s, the house was occupied through 1930, when it became part of the James Lee Art Academy, a precursor to the Memphis Academy of Art. When the academy moved in 1959, the building became city property and stood vacant. Beginning in 1961, city residents raised funds to restore and refurnish the house with period furniture and accessories, and it opened as a museum in 1964. This was during the period of urban renewal that saw to the demolition of many of Memphis's other old homes, and some of the house's furnishings were taken from homes that were later demolished. Tours include all three floors and the basement; there is no elevator to access the different levels. This is a good stop if you are interested in antiques.

The **Magevney House** (198 Adams Ave., 901/526-1484, free admission first Saturday of each month 1pm-4pm) and the **Mallory-Neely House** (652 Adams Ave., 901/523-1484, www.memphismuseums.org, 10am-4pm Fri.-Sat., adults $7, seniors $5, youth $5) are two other historical homes in the district. The Magevney House is the oldest middle-class residence still standing in Memphis. It was built in 1836 by an Irish immigrant to the city, Eugene Magevney. The Mallory-Neely House is of the same vintage and is notable for the fact that it was not refurnished in more than 100 years and so remains remarkably true to the era in which it was built.

Memphis Brooks Museum of Art

Memphis's foremost art museum is located in Overton Park in midtown, a short drive from downtown. **Memphis Brooks Museum of Art** (1934 Poplar Ave., 901/544-6200, www.brooksmuseum.org, 10am-4pm Wed. and Fri., 10am-8pm Thurs, 10am-5pm Sat., 11am-5pm Sun., adults $7, seniors $6, students and youth 7 and older $3) is the largest fine-art museum in Tennessee, and its permanent collection includes 8,000 works of art. This includes ancient African and Asian art, as well as 14th century-present European art and 18th century-present American art. There are 29 galleries

A giant panda is one draw at the Memphis Zoo.

polar bears at the Memphis Zoo

at the Brooks, and special exhibitions have focused on the work of Annie Leibovitz, men's fashion in Africa, and the silver work of Paul de Lamerie, Activist Photographers of the Civil Rights Movement, and American Folk Art. There is also a museum shop and restaurant, as well as an auditorium often used to screen films.

Memphis Zoo

The **Memphis Zoo** (2000 Prentiss Pl., 901/333-6500, www.memphiszoo. org, 9am-5pm daily Mar.-Oct., 9am-4pm daily Nov.-Feb., adults $15, children $10) has been expanding and is now the proud steward of two giant pandas, Le Le and Ya Ya; large cats; penguins; lions; tropical birds; and 3,500 other animal species. More hippos have been born here than at any other zoo. Its butterfly exhibit, open May-October, is a popular feature, and camel rides are available in the spring. The zoo is located on the grounds of Overton Park. Parking is an additional $5 and a point of some contention in the neighborhood. (Parking on the grass during zoo events upsets those who use the magnificent Overton Park for other events and purposes. Be mindful when you visit.)

Tennessee residents with ID can get in free on Tuesdays after 2pm, except in March; $3 fee for access to China/panda exhibit.

SOUTH MEMPHIS
★ Stax Museum of American Soul Music

Perhaps there is no place in Memphis that better tells the story of the city's legendary soul music than the **Stax Museum of American Soul Music** (926 E. McLemore Ave., 901/942-7685, www.staxmuseum.com, 10am-5pm Tues.-Sat. and 1pm-5pm Sun., additionally, 1pm-5pm Mon. Apr.-Oct., adults $12, seniors, students, and military $11, children 9-12 $9).

The museum tour starts with a short toe-tapping video that sets the scene for the musical magic that took place here during the 1960s. Exhibits include the sanctuary of an old clapboard Delta church, which illustrates the connection between soul and gospel music. You can also see Booker T. Jones's original organ, Otis Redding's favorite suede jacket, and Isaac Hayes's 1972 peacock-blue gold-trimmed Cadillac Eldorado, Superfly.

The museum also takes you through the studio's control room and into the studio itself, slanted floors and all. If you want to try your hand at singing, there is a karaoke machine, as well as a dance floor in case you can't help but move to the music. The Stax Museum is a must-see for music enthusiasts but also an educational journey for those who don't know the story behind some of America's most famous songs. It sits next door to the Stax Music Academy, a present-day music school that reaches out to neighborhood youth.

★ Graceland

Drive south from downtown on Elvis Presley Boulevard to reach the King's most famous home, **Graceland** (3717 Elvis Presley Blvd., 901/332-3322 or 800/238-2000, www.graceland.com or www.elvis.com, 9am-5pm Mon.-Sat., 9am-4pm Sun., Mar.-Oct., 10am-4pm daily Nov., 9 am-4pm Wed.-Mon. Dec., 10am-4pm Wed.-Mon. Jan-Feb., adults $36, seniors and students $32.40, children 7-12 $16, children 6 and under free). There is plenty of parking. Reservations are recommended.

Visitors can choose from five tour packages: The mansion-only tour takes about an hour and costs $36; the platinum tour includes the automobile museum, the Graceland Archives Experience and other special perks for $40. Platinum plus, at $45, adds Elvis's airplanes. Enthusiasts can choose one of the VIP packages, which give you "front of the line" access, an all-day pass, keepsakes, and access to exclusive exhibits, such as 60 Years of Elvis introduced to the VIP tour in 2014: $72 without a tour of Elvis's airplanes and $77 includes the airplanes.

Actor and Elvis fan John Stamos narrates an interactive multimedia digital tour that gives you access to archival audio, video, and photographs.

The Graceland complex blends into the strip malls and fast-food joints that line the boulevard in this part of Memphis. The ticket counter, shops, and restaurants are located on the west side of the boulevard, and here you board a shuttle van that drives across the highway and up the curved drive to the Graceland mansion. Graceland managers may have taken full advantage of the commercial opportunities presented by the home that Elvis left behind, but they have not overdone it. The operation is laid-back, leaving the spotlight on Elvis and, of course, his fans, who travel to Memphis from around the world to visit.

The mansion tour is conducted by audio guide. It includes the ground floor of the mansion (the upstairs remains closed to the public) and several outbuildings that now house exhibits about Elvis's life and career. High points include watching the press conference Elvis gave after leaving the army, witnessing firsthand his audacious taste in decor, and visiting the meditation garden where Elvis, his parents, and his grandmother are buried. There is also a plaque in memory of Elvis's lost twin, Jesse Garon. The audio tour plays many of Elvis's songs, family stories remembered by Elvis's daughter Lisa Marie Presley, and several clips of Elvis speaking. In 2015, Graceland opened two new exhibits: *Elvis: That's the Way It Is*, a documentary chronicling the legend's first Las Vegas performance, and "I Shot Elvis," which features photos from the early years of his career and encourages museum guests to take a photo with a larger-than image of the King.

The exhibits gloss over some of the challenges Elvis faced in his life—his addiction to prescription drugs, his womanizing and failed marriage, and his unsettling affinity for firearms among them. But they showcase Elvis's generosity, his dedication to family, and his fun-loving character. The portrait that emerges is sympathetic and remarkably human for a man who is so often portrayed as larger than life.

The automobile museum features 33 vehicles, including his pink Cadillac, motorcycles, and a red MG from *Blue Hawaii,* as well as some of his favorite motorized toys, including a go-kart and dune buggy. His private planes include the *Lisa Marie,* which Elvis customized with gold-plated seat belts, suede chairs, and gold-flecked sinks. Other special Graceland exhibits include "Sincerely Elvis," which chronicles Elvis's life in 1956, and "Elvis After Dark," which describes some of Elvis's late-night passions, like roller skating.

The Graceland mansion was declared a National Historic Site in 2006. It attracts more than 650,000 visitors annually. Expansion plans include the 450-room hotel/500-seat theater, Guest House at Graceland.

★ Elmwood Cemetery

Elmwood Cemetery (824 S. Dudley St., 901/774-3212, www.elmwood-cemetery.org, 8am-4:30pm daily), an 80-acre cemetery southwest of the city center, is the resting place of 70,000 Memphians—ordinary citizens and some of the city's most prominent leaders. It was founded in 1852 by

Nothing, especially not the pool room, is understated at Graceland Mansion.

Soulsville

A lucky convergence of people, talents, and social forces led to one of Memphis's—and America's—most distinctive musical stories. **Stax Records** was founded in 1960 by Jim Stewart, an aspiring country fiddler, and his sister, Estelle Axton. The first two letters of the brother and sister's surnames came together to form Stax, a name now synonymous with the raw Memphis sound of performers like Rufus and Carla Thomas, Otis Redding, Sam and Dave, Isaac Hayes, Eddie Floyd, the Mar-Keys, the Staple Singers, and Booker T. & the MGs.

Stewart chose a closed movie theater in a working-class South Memphis neighborhood for his recording studio. He was on a tight budget, so he didn't bother to fix the sloped theater floor or angled walls, and the room's reverberating acoustics came to define the Memphis sound.

Motown was known as "Hitsville" for its smooth and palatable sound, so the artists at Stax began to call their neighborhood "Soulsville," a name that still refers to the area of South Memphis where Stax is located. The soul music that Stax recorded was raw and inventive, influenced by country, blues, gospel, and jazz.

The label's first hit was with WDIA-AM disc jockey Rufus Thomas and his daughter, Carla Thomas, who came in one day and recorded "Cause I Love You." The song became an overnight sensation.

Stax tapped into the talent of the neighborhood, and particularly the African American Booker T. Washington High School, which graduated such greats as the members of the Soul Children and the Mad Lads. As the Stax reputation developed, artists came from out of town to record, including a 21-year-old Otis Redding, who drove up from Georgia in hopes of making a record and made a career instead.

Stax also operated **Satellite Records,** right next door to the studio, and here Estelle Axton was able to quickly test-market new recordings on the neighborhood youngsters who came in for the latest music. Wayne Jackson, a member of the studio's house band, the Memphis Horns, recalls that Estelle and Jim would invite hundreds of young people from the neighborhood into the studio to listen to their newest recording. Based on the group's response, they would choose the single.

Stax was unique for its time as an integrated organization, where the love of music trumped racial differences. As the civil rights movement evolved, Stax artists turned to serious social themes in their music. In 1972, Stax artists organized **WattStax,** an outdoor black music festival in Los Angeles.

Between 1960 and 1975, when the Stax magic ran out, the studio produced 800 singles and 300 albums, including 243 Top 100 and 14 number-one R&B hits. Isaac Hayes's theme from the movie *Shaft* was the fastest-selling album in Stax history, and one of three Stax songs went to number one on the pop charts. Other big Stax hits were Otis Redding's "(Sittin' on) The Dock of the Bay," the Staples Singers' "Respect Yourself," and Sam and Dave's "Soul Man."

Sadly, Stax was destroyed financially by a bad distribution deal with CBS Records in 1975, and the studio was closed. Its rare master tapes were sold at auction, and the studio where soul was born was demolished.

Thankfully, the story of Stax has not been forgotten. In 2001, ground was broken for a new Stax story, one that grew into the present-day music academy and the **Stax Museum of American Soul Music.**

50 gentlemen who wanted the cemetery to be a park for the living as well as a resting place for the dead. They invested in tree planting and winding carriage paths so that the cemetery today is a pleasant, peaceful place to spend a few hours.

The cemetery is the resting place of Memphians like Annie Cook, a well-known madam who died during the yellow fever epidemic of 1878; Marion Scudder Griffen, a pioneering female lawyer and suffragette; and musician Sister Thea Bowman. Thousands of anonymous victims of the yellow fever epidemic were buried here, as were both Confederate and Union casualties of the Civil War. Prominent citizens, including Robert Church Sr., Edward Hull Crump, and Shelby Foote, are also buried at Elmwood.

Visitors to the cemetery may simply drive or walk through on their own. But it is best to rent the one-hour audio guide ($10) of the cemetery, which takes you on a driving tour and highlights 50 people buried in the cemetery. Thanks to a well-written and well-presented narration, the cemetery tour comes closer than any other single Memphis attraction to bringing Memphis's diverse history and people to life.

The cemetery offers occasional lectures and docent-guided tours for $15. Call ahead or check the website to find out if any are scheduled during your visit. To find Elmwood, drive east along E. H. Crump Boulevard, turning south (right) onto Dudley, which dead-ends at the single-lane bridge that marks the entrance to the cemetery.

Tours are of the 1,500 trees in the Carlisle S. Page Arboretum are also available.

Church of the Full Gospel Tabernacle

A native of Arkansas and longtime resident of Michigan, Al Green first made his name as one of history's greatest soul singers, with hits like "Let's Stay Together," "Take Me to the River," and "Love and Happiness." Following a religious conversion in 1979, he dedicated his considerable

Elmwood Cemetery is the resting place of both famous and everyday Memphians.

Hale Rd., 901/396-9192) in Memphis, where his Sunday sermons dripped
with soulful gospel.

For almost 11 years, the Reverend Al Green left secular music, dedicat-
ing himself to God's music. He began his return to secular music in 1988
and in 1995 Green released the first of three new secular albums on Blue
Note Records.

According to his official biography, *Take Me to the River*, Reverend Green
faced some criticism when he returned to the secular scene. "I've got people in the church saying, 'That's a secular song,' and I'm saying, 'Yeah, but
you've got Monday, Tuesday, Wednesday, Thursday, Friday, and Saturday
to be anything other than spiritual. You've got to live those days, too!'"
Reverend Green writes. In the book he says he has not neglected his duty
to God: "The music is the message, the message is the music. So that's my
little ministry that the Big Man upstairs gave to me—a little ministry called
love and happiness."

Despite his rebirth as a secular soul performer, Al Green, now a bishop,
still makes time for his church. He preaches regularly, but not every
Sunday, and continues to sing the praises of God. The Sunday service at
his Memphis church begins at 11:30am. Visitors are welcome, and you can
come—within reason—as you are. Please show respect, though, by being
quiet when it's called for and throwing a few bucks in the offering plate
when it comes around. And don't forget that the church is a place of wor-
ship and not a tourist attraction. If you're not in town on Sunday, you can
catch the weekly choir rehearsal on Thursday at 7pm.

National Ornamental Metal Museum

An unusual delight, the **National Ornamental Metal Museum** (374 Metal
Museum Dr., 901/774-6380, www.metalmuseum.org, 10am-5pm Tues.-Sat.,
noon-5pm Sun., adults $6, seniors $5, students and children $4) is dedi-
cated to preserving and displaying fine metalwork. Its permanent collection
numbers more than 3,000 objects and ranges from contemporary American
sculpture to works up to 500 years old. The museum hosts special exhibits
several times a year, showcasing various aspects of metalwork. There is also
a working metalwork studio, and the museum grounds on the bluff overlooking the Mississippi are an attraction in themselves. This is reputed to
be the site where Spanish explorer Hernando de Soto and his men camped
when they passed through the area in 1542. Demonstrations may be available on weekend afternoons; call the museum in advance to confirm.

C. H. Nash Museum at Chucalissa

A group of platform and ridge mounds along the Mississippi River are the
main attraction at **Chucalissa Archaeological Site** (1987 Indian Village
Dr., 901/785-3160, www.memphis.edu/chucalissa, 9am-5pm Tues.-Sat.,
1pm-5pm Sun., adults $5, seniors and children $3). The mounds were
once part of a Choctaw Indian community that existed AD 1000-1550.

The village was empty when Europeans arrived, and the name *Chucalissa* means abandoned house.

The largest mound would have been where the chief and his family lived. The present-day museum, operated by the University of Memphis, consists of an exhibit about the Native Americans of the area and a self-guided tour around the mounds and courtyard area, where games and meetings would have been held. There is also a 0.5-mile nature trail along the bluff overlooking the river.

EAST MEMPHIS

East Memphis is home to old suburbs, gracious homes, and some excellent parks and other attractions.

The Dixon Gallery and Gardens

The Dixon Gallery and Gardens (4339 Park Ave., 901/761-5250, www. dixon.org, 10am-5pm Tues.-Sat., 1pm-5pm Sun., adults $7, seniors $5, children $3), an art museum housed inside a stately Georgian-style home, has an impressive permanent collection of more than 2,000 paintings, many of them French impressionist and postimpressionist style, including works by Monet, Renoir, Degas, and Cézanne. It also mounts a half-dozen special exhibits each year; previous ones have showcased the art of Lester Julian Merriweather, Rodin, and Brian Russell.

The Dixon is an easy place to spend several hours, immersed first in art and then in walking the paths that explore the house's 17 acres of beautifully tended gardens. There is a cutting garden, woodland garden, and formal gardens, among others.

Admission to the Dixon is free on Saturday between the hours of 10am-noon, and pay what you wish on Tuesday.

Memphis Botanic Garden

The 100-acre **Memphis Botanic Garden** (750 Cherry Rd., 901/636-4100, www.memphisbotanicgarden.com, 9am-6pm daily summer, 9am-4:30pm daily winter, adults $8, seniors $6.50, children $5) is home to more than 140 different species of trees and more than two dozen specialty gardens, including a Sculpture Garden, Azalea Trail, and Iris Garden. Trails meander through the gardens, but for the greatest fun buy a handful of fish food and feed the fish and ducks that inhabit the pond at the Japanese Garden. The garden puts on a number of events, including blockbuster concerts, workshops, plant sales, wine tastings, and programs for children. **Fratelli's Café** (901/766-9900, 11am-2pm daily) is a good option for lunch onsite.

The Pink Palace

A good destination for families, the Pink Palace (3050 Central Ave., 901/636-2362, www.memphismuseums.org, 9am-5pm Mon.-Sat., noon-5pm Sun.) is a group of attractions rolled into one. The **Pink Palace Museum** (adults $12.75, seniors $12.25, children $7.25, free after 1pm

Tues.) is a museum about Memphis, with exhibits about the natural history of the Mid-South region and the city's development. There is a full-scale replica of the first Piggly Wiggly supermarket, plus an exhibit about how health care became such a large part of the Memphis economy. The museum is housed within the Pink Palace Mansion, the Memphis home of Piggly Wiggly founder Clarence Saunders.

The Pink Palace is also home to the **Sharpe Planetarium,** which at this writing was closed for $1.5 million renovations. When complete it will include a newly upgraded 3D movie theater with daily screenings. Special package tickets are available for all the Pink Palace attractions.

The annual Enchanted Forest, a holiday-themed village and Christmas destination for families, is open mid-November through December 31. It has a separate or additional entry fee ($6 adults, $5 seniors and children under 12); proceeds benefit Le Bonheur Children's Hospital.

Art Museum of the University of Memphis

The **Art Museum of the University of Memphis** (142 CFA Building, 901/678-2224, www.memphis.edu/amum, 9am-5pm Mon.-Sat., free. Parking is free on weekends, otherwise $2 per hour in the parking garage) houses excellent but small exhibits of ancient Egyptian and African art and artifacts, and a noteworthy print gallery. There are frequent special exhibitions. The museum is closed during university holidays and in between temporary exhibits.

Children's Museum of Memphis

You will know the **Children's Museum of Memphis** (2525 Central Ave., 901/458-2678, www.cmom.com, 9am-5pm daily, $12) by the large alphabet blocks outside spelling its acronym, CMOM. Bring children here for constructive and educational play: They can sit in a flight simulator and real airplane cockpit, climb through the arteries of a model heart, climb a skyscraper, and more. The museum has 26 permanent exhibits and several traveling exhibits. Beat the Memphis summer heat at the museum's **H2Oh! Splash** park ($12 alone or $20 total combined with museum entry), which has 40 water sprayers in which children can frolic.

Davies Manor Plantation

Explore 32 acres of land and see the oldest log home in Shelby County open to the public at **Davies Manor Plantation,** (3570 Davieshire Dr., Bartlett, daviesmanorplantation.org, noon-4pm Tues.-Sat., Apr.-mid-Dec., adults $5, seniors $4, children and students $3, children 6 and under free) in suburban Bartlett. This historic plantation site includes a cotton patch, slave cabins, Civil War markers, and other artifacts left behind from a very different time in our nation's history. Davies Manor is likely not worth a trip on its own, but if you are traveling in the area, it is worth a stop. Special events include quilt shows.

Lichterman Nature Center

Lichterman Nature Center (5992 Quince Rd., 901/636-2211, www.memphismuseums.org/lichterman-overview, 10am-3pm Tues.-Thurs., 10am-4pm Fri.-Sat., adults $6, seniors $5.50, children $4.50) is dedicated to generating interest and enthusiasm for the Mid-South's nature. The park encompasses some 65 acres, and visitors will enjoy seeing native trees and flowers, including dogwood, lotus, and pine. There is a museum about the local environment, picnic facilities, and pleasant trails. Environmental education is the center's mission, and this certified arboretum is a popular destination for families and school groups.

TOURS

History Tours

Heritage Tours of Memphis (901/527-3427, www.heritagetoursofmemphis.com, adults $35, youth 12-17 $27, children 4-11 $25) is the city's only tour company dedicated to presenting Memphis's African American history. Operated by Memphians Elaine Turner and Joan Nelson, Heritage Tours offers black heritage, musical heritage, civil rights, and Beale Street walking tours. The company can also arrange out-of-town tours to area attractions, such as the **Alex Haley Museum and Interpretive Center** in Henning, Tennessee (adults $35, youth $30). Most local tours last about three hours.

The black heritage tour starts at the W. C. Handy Home and Museum and includes a stop at the Slavehaven Underground Railroad Museum plus narration that tells the story of black Memphians such as Ida B. Wells, Robert Church, and Tom Lee, and the events leading up to the assassination of Dr. Martin Luther King Jr. You will drive past the Mason Temple Church of God in Christ at 930 Mason Street, where Dr. King gave his famous "mountaintop" speech the night before his death.

River Tours

The **Memphis Queen Riverboat Tours** (901/527-2628, www.memphisriverboats.net, adults $20, seniors, college students, military, children 13-17 $17, children 4-12 $10, toddlers $5) leave daily at 2:30pm from the Port of Memphis, located at the foot of Monroe Avenue on the riverfront. The afternoon tour lasts 90 minutes and takes you a few miles south of the city before turning around. Commentary tells some of the most famous tales of the river, but the biggest attraction of the tour is simply being on Old Man River. The views of the Memphis skyline from the water are impressive. Concessions are available onboard. The riverboats also offer dinner cruises at 7:30pm with live music for about $45 per person. See website to check dates and times.

Music Tours

Music-themed tours are the specialty at **Backbeat Tours** (901/527-9415, www.backbeattours.com, $15-51, tickets must be reserved in advance). You will travel on a reconditioned 1959 transit bus and be serenaded by live musicians. Tours include the Memphis Mojo Tour (adults $28, students $26, children 7-12 $15), which takes you to Memphis music landmarks like Sun Studio and the Stax Museum, and the Hound Dog tour, which follows in Elvis Presley's Memphis footsteps. Backbeat can also take you to Graceland and offers two walking tours of Memphis—a Memphis Ghost Tour ($20 adult/$13 child) which explores the bloody and creepy side of history—and a Memphis historic walking tour (adult $15, child $9) both daily March-October and Saturdays only November and February.

Entertainment and Events

Memphis's vibrant, diverse personality is reflected in its entertainment scene. Blues, rap, R&B, and gospel are just some of the types of music you can hear on any given weekend. Alternative and indie rock finds a receptive audience in Memphis, as does opera, Broadway productions, and the symphony. There's always a good excuse to go out.

LIVE MUSIC AND CLUBS

Memphis may be the birthplace of the blues, but there's a lot more to the music scene than that. It's true that you can catch live blues at a Beale Street nightclub or in a city juke joint. But you can also find hard-edge rock, jazz, and acoustic music most nights of the week. The best resource for up-to-date entertainment listings is the free weekly *Memphis Flyer* (www.memphisflyer.com), which comes out on Wednesday morning and includes a detailed listing of club dates and concerts.

Keep in mind that big-name artists often perform at casinos in Tunica, just over the state line in Mississippi. Many of these shows are advertised in Memphis media outlets, or check out the upcoming events on the Tunica Convention and Visitors Bureau website, www.tunicamiss.com.

view of the Mississippi

Blues

One of the first things you should do when you get to Memphis is to find out if the **Center for Southern Folklore** (119 S. Main St., 901/525-3655, www. southernfolklore.com, Sun.-Thurs. noon-8, am, 11am-11pm Fri.-Sat.) has concerts or activities planned during your stay. The center has been documenting and preserving traditional Memphis and Delta blues music since the 1970s. The free self-guided tour of all things traditional-Southern leads you through Heritage Hall. This is also the location of concerts, lectures, and screenings of documentaries; they offer group tours and educational programs, and host the annual Memphis Music and Heritage Festival over Labor Day weekend. It often has live blues on Friday afternoon and offers a variety of special shows. This is one of the best places to hear authentic blues. The folklore store sells folk art, books, CDs, and traditional Southern food, and often hosts live music on Friday and Saturday nights. A sign stating "Be Nice or Leave" sets the tone as soon as you step into this colorful and eclectic shop, one of the best gift shops in the city. The center is a non-profit organization and well worth supporting. You'll find live music in the Folklore Store most Friday and Saturday nights starting around 8pm.

Beale Street is ground zero for Memphis's blues music scene. While some people lament that Beale has become a sad tourist shell of its former self, it can still be a worthwhile place to spend your evening. Indeed, no other part of Memphis has as much music and entertainment encompassing such a small area. On a typical night, Beale Street is packed with a diverse crowd strolling from one bar to the next. Beer seems to run a close second to music as the street's prime attraction, with many bars selling directly onto the street through concession windows. The "Big Ass Beer" cups used by many establishments say it all.

Nearly all Beale Street bars have live music, but one of the most popular is **B. B. King's Blues Club** (143 Beale St., 901/524-5464, www.bbkingclubs.com/memphis, Sun.-Thurs. 11am-midnight, Fri.-Sat. 11am-2am, on weekends typically there is a $3-5 cover, rarely on weekdays), owned by the legend himself. B. B. King performs here two or three times a year—keep your ear to the ground since the shows are not usually advertised. On other evenings, local acts and some nationally known performers take the stage. B. B. King's draws a mostly tourist crowd, and it is a chain, but with the blues on full throttle, you probably won't care too much.

Also on Beale Street, **Blues City Café** (138 Beale St., 901/526-3637, www. bluescitycafe.com, Sun.-Thurs. 11am-3am, Fri.-Sat. 11am-5am, cover $3-5) books blues, plus a variety of other acts including doo-wop, zydeco, R&B, funk, and "high-impact rockabilly." The café-restaurant is one of the most popular on Beale Street, and its nightclub, **Rum Boogie Café** (rumboogie. com, 11am–2am daily, cover $3-5), has an award-winning house band, James Covan and the Boogie Blues Band, that performs most evenings.

Jazz

If you want a break from the blues, **King's Palace Café** (162 Beale St.,

Memphis Juke Joints

In Memphis, there are only two reasons to go to a juke joint full of blues: because you feel good or because you feel bad. Beale Street is a reliable source seven nights a week, and your visit to Memphis wouldn't be complete without checking out its scene. But if you want to sneak away from the tourist crowd and catch some homegrown talent, check out a real Memphis juke joint. Live music is typical on Friday and Saturday nights and sometimes Sunday, but it gets scarce during the week. Generally music starts late (11pm) and finishes early (3am). Don't be surprised if the person you've engaged in conversation sitting next to you gets called to the stage sometime during the evening and delivers a beautiful song.

Remember that it's in the nature of things for these clubs to come and go. The following listings were current as of this writing, but they are always subject to change.

· **Wild Bill's** (1580 Vollintine Ave., 901/207-3075): A legendary club in Memphis. The Patriarch himself passed away in the summer of 2007, but what he established will still carry on. The quintessential juke joint. Small, intimate, an open kitchen serving chicken wings, and ice-cold beer served in 40-ounce bottles. Home to Ms. Nikki and the Memphis Soul Survivors.

· **CC's Blues Club** (1427 Thomas St., 901/526-5566): More upscale. More mirrors. But a great dance floor, and don't you dare come underdressed. Security guards patrol the parking lot.

· **Mr. Handy's Blues Hall** (182 Beale St., 901/528-0150): New Orleans has Preservation Hall. Memphis has Handy's Blues Hall. Everyone bad-raps Beale Street and its jangly tourism scene, but if you catch it on a good night, when Dr. Feelgood warms up his harmonica and you look around the room at the memorabilia on the walls, you could be in a joint at the end of a country road in Mississippi.

901/521-1851, Mon.-Thurs. 11am-10pm, Fri.-Sat. 11am-10:30pm, Sun. 11am-9:30pm, www.kingspalacecafe.com) specializes in jazz. Lots of wood paneling and red paint make the bar and Cajun restaurant warm and welcoming. This is an unpretentious place to have a meal or listen to live music. There is a $1 per person entertainment charge when you sit at a table.

Rock

Still on Beale Street, **Alfred's** (197 Beale St., 901/525-3711, www.alfredsonbeale.com, Sun.-Thurs. 11am-3am, Fri.-Sat. 11am-5am, cover $5 Fri. and Sat.) has rock acts five nights a week. On Sunday evening, the 17-piece Memphis Jazz Orchestra takes the stage. The dance floor at Alfred's is one of the best on Beale Street.

One of Beale Street's most historic concert venues, **The New Daisy** (330 Beale St., 901/525-8981, newdaisy.com, box office Tues. and Fri. 10am-6pm, Sat. noon-4pm, cover $10 and up, ticket costs vary) books rock 'n' roll, independent, and a few R&B acts. There are shows most nights of the week; call ahead or check the entertainment listings for a schedule. The Daisy is an all-ages club, and many shows attract a young audience.

Off Beale Street, the **Hi-Tone Café** (412-414 N. Cleveland, 901/490-0335, daily 5pm-3am, www.hitonememphis.com, cover varies, $2 charge for under 21) is probably the best place to see live music in town. The Hi-Tone books all kinds of acts, from high-energy rockers to soulful acoustic acts. They are really committed to bringing good live music to Memphis. The cover charge for local shows is a few bucks, but tickets for bigger-name acts can run $20 and more. The bar serves respectable burgers and finger foods, excellent martinis, and lots of beer.

Also in Midtown, **The Buccaneer** (1368 Monroe, 901/278-0909, daily 5pm-3am, cover varies) books rock acts most days a week. Cover charge rarely tops $5.

BARS
Downtown

You can head to Beale Street for a night out, regardless of whether or not you sing the blues.

The best place to grab a beer downtown is the **Beale Street Tap Room** (168 Beale St., 901/521-1851). With more than 30 beers on tap, this is a great choice for beer lovers. The service is friendly and low-key, and regulars have their own mug.

Off Beale Street, **The Peabody Hotel Memphis** (149 Union Ave., 901/529-4000, www.peabodymemphis.com) may be the best place to enjoy a relaxing drink. The lobby bar offers good service, comfortable seats, and an unrivaled atmosphere.

On Peabody Place, about a block from Beale Street, the **Flying Saucer Draught Emporium** (130 Peabody Pl., 901/523-8536, www.beerknurd.com) draws a lively happy-hour crowd. The bar offers more than 75 draft beers, plus cocktails and wine. Grab a seat along the windows and watch downtown Memphis come alive as the sun sets.

In the South Main district, **Ernestine and Hazel's** (531 S. Main St., 901/523-9754, earnestineandhazelsjukejoint.com) is one of Memphis's most celebrated pit stops for cold drinks and a night out. Once a brothel, Ernestine and Hazel's now has one of the best jukeboxes in town. Take a seat upstairs in one of the old brothel rooms and watch South Main Street below. Rumor is the joint is haunted, but folks come here for the jukebox, not the spirits.

If beer's your thing, check out the growler station at **Joe's Wine & Beer** (1681 Poplar Ave., 901/725-4252, joeswinesandliquor.com). Behind this iconic signage you'll find 20 beer taps and 10 wine taps.

Midtown

The **Young Avenue Deli** (2119 Young Ave., 901/278-0034, www.youngavenuedeli.com, daily 11am-3am, kitchen closes at 2am) is a friendly neighborhood bar that books occasional live acts. Located in the hip Cooper-Young neighborhood, Young Avenue Deli has hundreds of different beers on tap or in bottles. The bar attracts a diverse crowd, from young hipsters to older neighborhood denizens.

A favorite place for music, pool, and a night out in midtown is the **Blue Monkey** (2012 Madison Ave., 901/272-2583, www.bluemonkeymemphis. com, daily 11am-3am). Grab a pizza and a beer, shoot some pool, and then rock out to the live band. There's a second location downtown (513 S. Front St., 901/527-6665).

Murphy's (1589 Madison Ave., 901/726-4193, www.murphysmemphis. com, Mon.-Sat. 11am-3am, Sun. noon-3am) is a neighborhood bar with a nice patio.

Perfect for a business date or after-work pit stop, **The Grove Grill** (4550 Poplar Ave., 901/818-9951, www.thegrovegrill.com, Sun.-Thurs. 11am-9pm, Fri.-Sat. 11am-10pm) is popular with businesspeople and office workers.

Two of Memphis's best sports bars are found in the eastern reaches of the city. **Brookhaven Pub & Grill** (695 W. Brookhaven Cir., 901/680-8118, www.brookhavenpubandgrill.com, daily 11am-2am) has big-screen plasma televisions, great beer on tap, and lots of fans. Tuesday night is Team Trivia night.

There's more to do than just watch the game at **Rec Room** (3000 Broad Ave., 901/209-1137, recroommemphis.com, 4pm-midnight Mon.-Thurs., 4pm-2am Fri., 11am-2am Sat., 11am-midnight Sun.). In addition to oversized screens for sports-watching, you can also get your game on with vintage video games, board games, and tabletop games such as foosball and Ping-Pong. Though Rec Room doesn't have a menu of its own, food trucks regularly pull up to the patio to tend to customers' cravings. Kids are welcome before 5pm if escorted by an adult; after 5pm, it's 18 and up.

A modern reboot of a historic music venue, **Lafayette's Music Room** (2119 Madison Ave. 901/207-5097, lafayettes.com/memphis, 11am-10:30pm Mon.-Wed., 11am-midnight Thurs., 11am-2am Fri.-Sat., 11am-midnight Sun., $15-24) features live music every night, a two-story patio and Southern-inspired fare.

GAY AND LESBIAN NIGHTLIFE

Many Memphis gay and lesbian clubs don't get going until late night, after other clubs have closed.

Dru's Place (1474 Madison Ave., 901/275-8082, www.drusplace.com, Sun.-Thurs. 1pm-midnight, Fri.-Sat. 1pm-2am) is a welcoming bar that has weekly Drag Time and Beer Bust. The beer is cold and the liquor is BYO.

Club Spectrum Memphis (600-616 Marshall Ave., 901/292-2292, Fri.-Sat. 9pm-4am) is a gay-, lesbian-, and everyone-welcome dance club. This is a weekend-only spot to get your groove on.

The Pumping Station (1382 Poplar Ave., 901/272-7600, thepumpingstationmemphis.com, Mon.-Fri. 4pm-3am, Sat.-Sun. 3pm-3am) is one of the city's favorite gay bars, with a full bar, craft beers on tap, and an outdoor beer garden (called The Backdoor Lounge, which is the only place you can smoke). It is housed in a building that once allowed a Jewish couple, evicted from another location, to open a liquor store, and is proud of its inclusive historical roots.

THE ARTS

Memphis has a growing arts scene. **ArtsMemphis** (901/578-2787, www.artsmemphis.org) provides funding for more than 20 local arts groups and is a reliable source of information about upcoming events.

Major arts venues include the **Cannon Center for the Performing Arts** (255 N. Main St., 901/576-1200, www.thecannoncenter.com) and the **Orpheum Theatre** (Main and Beale Sts. 203 S. Main St, 901/525-3000, www.orpheum-memphis.com). They regularly book major artists and Broadway performances.

Theater

For theater, check out **Playhouse on the Square** (66 S. Cooper St., 901/726-4656, www.playhouseonthesquare.org). This dynamic Memphis institution serves as home to several of the city's acting companies and puts on 15-20 different performances every year. It also offers theater classes, school performances, and pay-what-you-can shows.

Theatre Memphis (630 Perkins Ext., 901/682-8323, www.theatrememphis.org) is a community theater company that has been in existence since the 1920s. It stages about 12 shows annually at its theater in midtown.

TheatreWorks (2085 Monroe Ave., 901/274-7139, www.theatreworks-memphis.org) and **Evergreen Theatre** (1705 Poplar Ave., 901/274-7139) encourage nontraditional and new theater with organizations, including Our Own Voice Theatre Troupe; Bluff City Tri-Art Theatre Company; Cazateatro, Emerald Theatre Company; FreakEngine; Inner City South; New; Threepenny Theatre, and others.

Catch a show at the Cannon Center for the Performing Arts.

The **Memphis Symphony Orchestra** (585 S. Mendenhall Rd., 901/537-2525, www.memphissymphony.org) performs on a varied calendar of works year-round in its home at the Cannon Center for the Performing Arts at 2155 North Main Street. The symphony was founded in 1952 and today has more than 850 musicians, staff, and volunteers.

Opera

Opera Memphis (6745 Wolf River Blvd., 901/257-3100, www.operamemphis.org) performs traditional opera at a variety of venues around town, including the historic Playhouse on the Square and the Germantown Performing Arts Centre. For the 30 days of September the company performs "pop-up" operas at different locations around the city.

Dance

Ballet Memphis (901/737-7322, www.balletmemphis.org) performs classical dance at the Playhouse on the Square, the Orpheum and other venues throughout the city. The **New Ballet Ensemble** (901/726-9225, www.new-ballet.org) puts on performances around the city with "dancers in do-rags as well as tights," in the words of the *Commercial Appeal.*

Cinemas

There are a half-dozen multiscreen movie theaters in and around Memphis. For independent movies, try **Malco's Paradiso** (584 S. Mendenhall Rd., 901/682-1754, www.malco.com) or **Studio on the Square** (2105 Court St., 901/725-7151, www.malco.com). In the summer, check out the **Orpheum** (203 S. Main St., 901/525-3000) for classic movies, and the **Malco Summer 4 Drive-In** (5310 Summer Ave., 901/767-4320) for an outdoor movie-watching experience.

FESTIVALS AND EVENTS
Spring

Memphians celebrate their African heritage over a long weekend in mid-April. **Africa in April** (901/947-2133, www.africainapril.org) honors a specific country in Africa each year. Activities include cooking, storytelling, music, and a parade. The festival takes place at Church Park on the east end of Beale Street.

In early May, the Memphis-based Blues Foundation hosts the annual **Blues Music Awards** (www.blues.org), the Grammys of the blues world. Per the foundation, a nominee announcement, as well as ticket information for the event, is released each year in mid-December on their website.

Memphis in May (www.memphisinmay.org), the city's largest annual event, is really three major festivals rolled into one. The **Beale Street Music Festival,** which takes place at Tom Lee Park on the river, kicks things off with a celebration of Memphis music. Expect a lot of wow-worthy performers, plus many more up-and-coming talents. The festival has grown over the years, and it is now a three-day event with four stages of music going simultaneously. In addition to music, the festival offers excellent people-watching, lots of barbecue, cold beer, and festivity. You can buy daily tickets or a three-day pass for the whole weekend.

In mid-May, attention turns to the **World Championship Barbecue Cooking Contest,** a celebration of pork, pigs, and barbecue that takes place in Tom Lee Park. In addition to the barbecue judging, there is entertainment, hog-calling contests, and other piggy antics. If you're not part of a competing team (or friends with one), you can buy barbecue from vendors who set up in the park.

Finally, there's the **Memphis International Festival,** which pays tribute to a different country each year with presentations about its music, food, culture, and history.

A sunset symphony caps off the month-long festivities. Book your hotel rooms early for Memphis in May, since many hotels, particularly those in downtown, sell out.

Summer

Don't let the name fool you, **Carnival Memphis** (901/458-2500, www.carnivalmemphis.org) is a Mardi Gras-style celebration, not a fairgrounds-esque event. It features a parade, fireworks, a ball, and more. This festival, once called Cotton Carnival, was segregated for decades, but since the mid-1980s has been racially integrated. This celebration raises funds for local children's charities. Like carnivals elsewhere in the south, Carnival Memphis consists of several events, including the Crown & Sceptre Ball, Princess Ball, and a luncheon for businesses. Carnival members (who pledge $75-2500 in fees) get discounted tickets or tickets included in their membership, depending on their contribution. Public ticket prices are released annually on the website.

The annual candlelight vigil at Graceland on August 15, the anniversary of Elvis's death, has grown into a whole week of Elvis-centric activities throughout Memphis. More than 30,000 people visit Graceland during **Elvis Week** (www.elvisweek.com), and during the vigil his most adoring fans walk solemnly up the Graceland drive to pay their respects at his grave. Special concerts, tribute shows, and movies are shown during the week as the city celebrates its most famous son even more than usual.

Fall

Organized by the Center for Southern Folklore, the **Memphis Music and Heritage Festival** (901/525-3655, www.southernfolklore.com), held over Labor Day weekend, sticks close to the roots of Memphis music. Performers include gospel singers, bona fide bluesmen and women, rockabilly superstars, and much more. Performances take place in the center's shop and concert hall on Main Street, making them more intimate than other blockbuster music festivals.

End-of-summer fairs are a tradition for Southern and rural communities all over the United States. The 10-day **Mid-South Fair** (901/274-8800, www.midsouthfair.org) in September is a bonanza of attractions: livestock shows, rodeos, agricultural judging, concerts, beauty pageants, exhibitions, carnival rides, funnel cakes, and cotton candy. The fair is held in northern Mississippi, about 30 miles south of Memphis.

In mid-September, the Cooper-Young neighborhood throws its annual jamboree at the **Cooper-Young Festival** (www.cooperyoungfestival.com). There is an arts and crafts fair, live music, and food vendors at this street carnival.

The annual **Southern Heritage Classic** (www.southernheritageclassic.com) is one of the South's big football games. But the match of two historically black college rivals, Jackson State University and Tennessee State University, is more than just a game, it is a serious citywide festival.

Forty-six-foot-long boats with dragon heads and tails race at Mud Island River Park each September during the **Duncan-Williams Dragon Boat Races** (www.memphis.racedragonboats.com). Proceeds benefit the work of the Tennessee Clean Water Network.

Winter

The colder weather welcomes a number of sporting events, including the **St. Jude Marathon and Half Marathon** (www.stjudemarathon.org, 800/565-5112) in December, which is a qualifying race for the Boston Marathon. The **AutoZone Liberty Bowl** (www.libertybowl.org, 901/795-7700) typically welcomes two of the National Collegiate Athletic Association's (NCAA) best football teams to town on New Year's Eve.

Taking place over the weekend closest to Elvis Presley's January 8 birthday, the **Elvis Birthday Celebration** (www.elvis.com) draws Elvis fans with special performances, dance parties, and a ceremony at Graceland proclaiming Elvis Presley Day.

ENTERTAINMENT AND EVENTS

The St. Jude Marathon gives runners a chance to run en masse on Beale Street.

Shopping

GIFTS AND SOUVENIRS

Any of the half-dozen shops along Beale Street sell gifts and souvenirs of the city. **Memphis Music** (149 Beale St., 901/526-5047, memphismusicstore. com) has a good selection of CDs and DVDs for music fans. For a unique gift or something practical for yourself, A. Schwab (163 Beale St., 901/523-9782, a-schwab.com) is your best choice and is lots of fun to boot.

Another good place for gift shopping is the **Center for Southern Folklore** (123 S. Main St., 901/525-3655), which has books, art, and music focusing on the region. All of the city's museums have good gift shops, including the **National Civil Rights Museum** (Sun. 1pm-5pm, Mon. and Wed.-Sat. 9am-5pm, closed Tuesday), **Stax Museum of American Soul Music** (Tues.-Sat. 10am-5pm, Sun. 1pm-5pm), and **Sun Studio** (daily 10am-6:15pm), where everything is emblazoned with the distinctive yellow Sun label.

If you have a car, head out to **Shangri-La Records** (1916 Madison Ave., 901/274-1916, www.shangri.com), one of the city's best record stores, which specializes in Memphis music. **Goner Records** (2152 Young Ave., 901/722-0095, Mon.-Sat. noon-7pm, Sun. 1pm-5pm, www.goner-records.com) is both a record store and a record label.

If the gift recipient in your life is a fashion maven, head to **Thigh High Jeans** (525 N. Main, www.thighhighjeans.com) where you can buy embroidered skirts and newly remade jeans created from recycled denim. A percentage of each purchase is donated to local, national and global charities. Or host a party with your friends and select the charity that is benefited.

ART

For art boutiques and galleries, head south to the South Main arts district, where you will find galleries, including **Robinson Gallery/Archives** (44

Shopping at Goner Records is a Memphis must.

Huling Ave., 901/619-4478, Mon.-Fri. 10am-5pm, closed Sat. and Sun., www.robinsongallery.com), a photography gallery that houses the work of *Vogue* photographer Jack Robinson, Jr.

On the last Friday of each month the trolleys are free, the galleries stay open, and hundreds of arts-minded Memphians head to South Main to mingle into the night. For a directory of all South Main galleries, contact the **South Main Association** (www.gosouthmain.com). The event starts at 6pm and runs "'til the musicians go home."

Since 2003 the **Wings Gallery** (100 N. Humphreys Blvd., 901/322-2984, Mon.-Fri. 8:30am-5pm, closed Sat. and Sun.) has shown the work of artists whose lives have been impacted by cancer. Exhibitions change every six weeks.

ANTIQUES

Head out to Central Avenue between Cooper and East Parkway for the greatest concentration of antiques stores. **Flashback** (2304 Central Ave., 901/272-2304, Mon.-Sat. 10:30am-5:30pm, Sun. 1pm-5pm, www.flashbackmemphis.com) sells both vintage furniture and clothes, including a whole lot of Levi's jeans. **Palladio Antiques and Arts** (2169 Central Ave., 901/276-3808, Mon.-Sat. 10am-5pm, closed Sunday www.thepalladiogroup.com) works with more than 75 dealers to provide a cross-section of styles for shoppers.

THRIFT STORES

In a city where vintage never went out of style, you can expect excellent thrift stores. The biggest and best is **AmVets** (2526 Elvis Presley Blvd., 901/775-5010, Mon.-Sat. 9am-9pm, Sun. 10am-6pm). You can also try the Junior League of Memphis's **Repeat Boutique Thrift Store** (3586 Summer Ave., 901/327-4777, 10am-5pm Tues.-Sat.).

In a city of characters, the most colorful shopping experience in Memphis is found at **The Memphis Flea Market—The Big One** (in the AgriCenter, 7777 Walnut Grove Rd., 901/276-3532, www.memphisfleamarket.com), which takes place the third weekend of most months, the exceptions are the fourth weekend of February and an extra market the first weekend of December) at the Mid-South Fairgrounds. Between 800 and 1,000 vendors turn up each month with housewares, clothing, computers, jewelry, antiques, yard art, and so much more. Between 20,000 and 25,000 people come to shop. Admission is $3 for adults, free for kids. Parking is free.

SHOPPING MALLS

The most upscale shopping mall in the Memphis area is **Wolfchase Galleria** (2760 N. Germantown Pkwy., 901/372-9409). Located in Cordova, an east-lying suburb now consumed by Memphis sprawl, the galleria is approaching its 20th anniversary. It is now showing its age but still attracts shoppers with national retailers, including Victoria's Secret, Disney, Fossil,

Gap, Coach, Abercrombie & Fitch, and Sephora. Department stores at the mall include Macy's, Dillard's, Sears, and JCPenney. You can take either exit 16 or 18 off I-40 to get to Wolfchase Galleria.

Also in Germantown, the swanky **Shops of Saddle Creek** (7509 Poplar Ave., 901/753-4264) has Anthropologie, Brooks Brothers, J. Crew, Vera Bradley, Talbots, Banana Republic, and an Apple computer store, among others.

Closer to the city center, **Oak Court Mall** (4465 Poplar Ave., 901/682-8928) was the location of the first Starbucks in Tennessee. It is also consistently voted Memphians' favorite mall, no doubt because it offers a good selection of stores in a pleasant atmosphere, and it's relatively close to town. Department stores at Oak Court include Macy's and Dillard's; the mall also has Godiva, JoS. A. Bank, Banana Republic, and dozens more stores.

And if that's not enough for you, head across the road to **Laurelwood Shopping Center** (Poplar Ave. at Perkins Ext., 901/682-8436), where you'll find bookstores, specialty clothing and shoe boutiques, as well as special events like free yoga classes.

In South Memphis, **Southland Mall** (1215 Southland Mall, 901/346-7664) is Memphis's oldest mall. Built in 1966 (it was the first enclosed mall in the Mid-South), Southland soldiers on. There is a Sears, as well as specialty shops, including Radio Shack and Bath & Body Works.

OUTLET SHOPPING

Opened in time for the 2015 holiday season, **Tanger Outlets** (5205 Airways Blvd., Southaven, MS, 662/349-1701www.tangeroutlet.com/southaven) has discounted outposts for more than 70 brands, including Michael Kors and LOFT.

Sports and Recreation

With a professional basketball team, excellent downtown baseball club, and lots of city parks, Memphis is a great city in which to both watch sports and get active yourself.

PARKS
Downtown

Named for the legendary blues composer W. C. Handy, **Handy Park,** on Beale Street, between 3rd Street and Rufus Thomas Boulevard, seems a tad out of place among Beale's nightclubs and restaurants. But the park is a site of historical importance, if only because of the statue of its namesake that guards its gates. The park hosts occasional outdoor concerts and festivals, and at other times you will find places to sit and a handful of vendors.

Uptown

Tom Lee Park, a long, 30-acre, narrow grassy park that overlooks the

Mississippi, is a popular venue for summertime festivals and events, including the Memphis in May BBQ Festival. It is also used year-round for walking and jogging and by people who simply want to look out at the giant river. The park is named for Tom Lee, an African American man who saved the lives of 32 people when the steamboat they were on sank in the river in 1925. Lee, who pulled people out of the river and into his boat, "Zev," could not even swim. An outmoded monument erected at the park in 1954 calls Lee "a very worthy negro."

Located on the northern side of downtown Memphis, **Court Square,** three blocks from the waterfront along Court Avenue, is a pleasant city park surrounded by historic buildings. Court Square is one of four parks that was included when the city was first planned in 1819. There are benches and trees, and it is a wireless Internet hot spot.

Memphis Park, located on Front Street between Court and Jefferson Streets, commemorates Civil War soldiers who died in the Battle of Memphis. There is a statue of Jefferson Davis in the center of the park. This is where many Memphians gathered to watch the Battle of Memphis in 1862, and it remains a good place to view the river below.

Midtown

Located in midtown Memphis, **Overton Park** (1928 Poplar Ave.) is one of the best all-around parks the city has to offer. This 342-acre park has a nine-hole golf course, nature trails through the woods, bike trails, an outdoor amphitheater now called the Levitt Shell, and lots of green, open spaces. The park shares space with the Memphis Zoo and the Memphis Brooks Museum of Art, making the area a popular destination for city residents and visitors. Patience may be required when looking for a parking spot during an event at Overton.

The Madison Avenue trolley passes **Forrest Park,** along Madison Avenue, between North Manassas and North Dunlap Streets, an ample city

Live music at Levitt Shell is a local favorite.

park dedicated to the memory of the controversial Nathan Bedford Forrest. Forrest, a slave trader, Confederate, and the first grand wizard of the Ku Klux Klan, has an uncomfortable position of prominence in Memphis and the whole of western Tennessee. Both he and his wife are buried in the park.

South Memphis

Southwest of the city center, about 15 minutes' drive from the airport, is **T. O. Fuller State Park** (1500 Mitchell Rd., 901/543-7581). The visitors center here is open weekdays 8am-sunset. Amenities at the 1,138-acre park include sheltered picnic areas, tennis courts, a golf course, a swimming pool ($3), basketball courts, a softball field, six miles of hiking trails, and camping facilities. T. O. Fuller State Park was the first state park east of the Mississippi River open to African Americans, and the second in the nation. An outdoor Environmental Interpretive Learning Center is in the planning stages at T. O. Fuller State Park.

East Memphis

Located near the University of Memphis and Oak Court Mall, **Audubon Park** (4161 Park Ave.) has a golf course, tennis courts, walking trails, and other sports facilities. The Memphis Botanic Garden is located here.

Memphians celebrate the fact that their largest city park, **Shelby Farms** (www.shelbyfarmspark.org), is five times the size of New York's Central Park. But the fact is that Shelby Farms is underused, because most of its 4,500 acres are pleasantly undeveloped. There are plans to improve the park by adding more recreational facilities: a new visitors center, retreat center, event pavilion, boat kiosk, and wetland walk with new trails are envisioned. A zip line is also in the works.

More than 500,000 people come here annually to go mountain biking, horseback riding, inline skating, walking, or running along some of the many trails. You can also fish, raft, canoe, or sail on any of the park's six lakes. There is a wheelchair-accessible trail, areas for picnicking, and a shooting range. Shelby Farms was originally set aside to be the county penal farm, and although it was not used in this way, the county jail is found on the western edge of the park. Shelby Farms is located on the eastern side of the city, just outside the I-40/I-240 loop that circles Memphis. It is easily accessible from exits 12 and 14 off I-40, and exit 13 off I-240. Or follow Walnut Grove Road from midtown.

BIKING

Most cyclists in the city bike as a form of recreation, rather than transportation. The City of Memphis has established five bike routes that circle the city and various neighborhoods. These routes are marked and have designated parking and restroom facilities at the start. They are not bike paths—you share the road with cars—and normal safety measures are necessary.

The **Memphis Hightailers Bicycle Club** (www.memphishightailers. com) organizes frequent rides for various levels, with distances ranging

20-100 miles. Regularly scheduled Urban Bicycle Food Ministry rides are listed for people to help distribute food while riding 10-12 miles. For bike rentals, gear, and advice about riding in and around the city, go to **Peddler Bike Shop** (3548 Walker Ave., 901/327-4833, Mon.-Wed. and Fri. 9am-6pm, Sat. 9am-5pm, Sun. 1pm-5pm, closed Thurs., www.peddlerbikeshop.com), where owner Hal Mabray will happily help you get geared up to ride. A used-bike rental will cost about $35 for a half day, $50 per day. Peddler also has locations in Germantown, Tennessee, and Southaven, Mississippi. Opt for a long weekend rate for just $100.

There are a number of parks near Memphis that are bike friendly. **Meeman-Shelby Forest State Park** (910 Riddick Road, 901/876-5215), north of the city, has five miles of paved bike paths, and cyclists use the main park roads for more extensive riding. Bicyclists will also find trails and bike rentals at **Shelby Farms.**

It is also noteworthy that the **Mississippi River Trail,** a bicycle route that runs 3,000 miles from the headwaters of the Mississippi River in Minnesota to the Gulf of Mexico, runs through Memphis and on to Mississippi. For maps and details, go to www.mississippirivertrail.org.

GOLF

The City of Memphis operates award-winning 18-hole golf courses at **Audubon Park** (4160 Park Ave., 901/683-6941), with gently rolling hills; **Fox Meadows** (3064 Clarke Rd., 901/362-0232), which is easy to walk but has several challenging holes; **Galloway Park** (3815 Walnut Grove, 901/685-7805); **Davy Crockett Golf Course** (4380 Rangeline Rd., 901/358-3375); and **Pine Hill Park** (1005 Alice Ave., 901/775-9434), a great course for walkers.

There are two public nine-hole courses: one at **Riverside Park** (465 S. Parkway W., 901/576-4296) and one at **Overton Park** (2080 Poplar Ave., 901/725-9905). Greens fees on the public courses are under $20.

The semiprivate Audubon-certified **Mirimichi** (6195 Woodstock Cuba Rd., 901/259-3800, www.mirimichi.com) in Millington is part-owned by heartthrob Justin Timberlake, a native (and still sometimes) Memphian. Millington is about a 30-minute drive from downtown.

TENNIS

The city operates public tennis courts at several parks, including **Bert Ferguson Park** (8495 Trinity) four outdoor, **Gaisman Park** (4221 Macon) two outdoor, **Glenview** (1885 Highway 78) two courts, **Martin Luther King Jr. Park (Riverside)** (South Pkwy. at Riverside Dr.) four lighted, **University Park** (University at Edward) four outdoor, **Audubon** (4145 Southern Ave.) four indoor/eight outdoor, **Frayser Park** (2907 N. Watkins) eight outdoor, **Hickory Hill** (3910 Ridgeway Rd.) 4 lighted, and **Pierotti** (3678 Powers Rd.) eight lighted (www.tennismemphis.org).

There are also four public indoor/outdoor tennis complexes: **Bellevue at Jesse Turner Park** (1239 Orgill Rd., 901/774-7199, Mon.-Thurs. 3pm-9pm, Fri. 3pm-7:3pm, Sat.-Sun. 9am-3pm); **Leftwich** (4145 Southern,

901/685-7907, Mon.-Fri. 7:30pm-9pm, Sat.-Sun 7:30am-7:30pm); **Whitehaven,** also called **Eldon Roark Tennis Center** (1500 Finley Rd., 901/332-0546, indoor courts Mon.-Thurs. 3pm-9pm, Fri. 3pm-7:30pm, Sat. 9am-6pm, Sun. noon-6pm, outdoor courts Mon.-Thurs. 9am-noon and 3pm-9pm, Fri. 9am-noon and 3pm-6pm, Sat. 9am-3pm, Sun. noon-6pm); and **Wolbrecht** (1645 Ridgeway, 901/767-2889, Mon.-Fri. 7:30am-9pm, Sat.-Sun. 7:30am-7:30pm). Fees vary per facility; call in advance for information and court reservations.

GYMS

Out-of-towners can get a day pass to the **Louis T. Fogelman Downtown YMCA** (245 Madison Ave., 901/527-9622, 5am-10pm Mon.-Thurs., 5am-8pm Fri., 7am-5pm Sat., noon-5pm Sun., day pass $10 to use the indoor pool and track, and extensive gym facilities). City residents can buy one of the membership packages.

SPECTATOR SPORTS
Basketball

In 2001, Memphis realized the dream of many in the Mid-South when the Vancouver Grizzlies announced they would be moving south. The National Basketball Association (NBA) team played its first two seasons in Memphis at the Pyramid before the massive $250 million FedEx Forum opened for the 2004-2005 season. The arena is one of the largest in the NBA and hosts frequent concerts and performances by major artists.

The **Grizzlies** have yet to achieve any major titles, but their finals and playoffs rankings keep fans coming back. Ticket prices range from under $20 to several hundred dollars. For ticket information, contact the **FedEx Forum box office** (191 Beale St., 901/205-2640, www.fedexforum.com, 10am-5:30pm Mon.-Fri.) or purchase through Ticketmaster. The NBA season runs October-April.

The Memphis Redbirds play at Autozone Park.

The **University of Memphis Tigers** surprised many in 2008 by making it all the way to the men's NCAA Championship. The team's remarkable 38-2 season brought new energy and excitement to the university's basketball program that continues today.

You can watch Tigers basketball November-April at FedEx Forum. Tickets are available from the FedEx Forum box office, or contact University of Memphis Athletics (www.gotigersgo.com) for more information.

Baseball

From April to October, the **Memphis Redbirds** (901/721-6000, www.memphisredbirds.com, $6-26) play AAA ball at the striking **AutoZone Park** in downtown Memphis. The stadium is bounded by Union Avenue, Madison Avenue, and 3rd Street, and is convenient to dozens of downtown hotels and restaurants. The Redbirds are an affiliate of the St. Louis Cardinals. Cheap tickets ($6) buy you a seat on the grassy berm, or you can pay a little more for seats in the stadium or boxes.

The Redbirds are owned by a nonprofit organization that also operates a number of community and youth programs in the city.

Racing

The **Memphis International Raceway** (550 Victory Ln., 901/969-7223, www.racemir.com) is located a short drive from downtown Memphis in Millington, northeast of the city center. The park includes a 0.75-mile NASCAR oval, a 0.25-mile drag racing strip, and a 1.77-mile road course. It hosts more than 200 race events every year, including a stop in the annual Busch Series races.

Millington is located about 30 minutes' drive north of Memphis. From the west, take I-40 E toward Nashville. From the east, take I-40 W toward Memphis.

Ice Hockey

The **RiverKings** (662/342-1755, www.riverkings.com, $5-30, Oct.-Apr.) play minor-league ice hockey at the **Landers Center** (4650 Venture Dr., Southaven, MS), about 20 miles south of Memphis off I-55.

Accommodations

There are thousands of cookie-cutter hotel rooms in Memphis, but travelers would be wise to look past major chains. If you can afford it, choose to stay in downtown Memphis. With the city at your doorstep, you'll have a better experience both day and night. Downtown is also where you'll find the most distinctive accommodations, including fine luxury hotels, charming inns, and an antebellum guest home.

Budget travelers have their pick of major chain hotels; the farther from the city center, the cheaper the room. Beware of very good deals, however, since you may find yourself in sketchy neighborhoods. There is a campground with tent and RV sites within a 15-minute drive of downtown at T. O. Fuller State Park.

DOWNTOWN
$150-200

The ★ **Talbot Heirs Guesthouse** (99 S. 2nd St., 901/527-9772, www.talbotheirs.com, $130-275), in the heart of downtown, offers a winning balance of comfort and sophistication. Each of the inn's eight rooms has its own unique decor—from cheerful red walls to black-and-white chic. All rooms are thoughtfully outfitted with a full kitchen and modern bathroom, television, radio and CD player, sitting area, desk, and high-speed Internet. Little extras, like the refrigerator stocked for breakfast, go a long way, as does the cheerful yet efficient welcome provided by proprietors Tom and Sandy Franck. Book early since the Talbot Heirs is often full, especially during peak summer months.

Over $200

In 2007, Memphis welcomed the **Westin Memphis Beale Street** (170 George W. Lee Ave., 901/334-5900, $195-369), located across the street from FedEx Forum and one block from Beale Street. The hotel's 203 guest rooms are plush and modern, each with a work desk, high-speed Internet, MP3-player docking station, and super-comfortable beds. The location can be noisy when Beale Street is in full swing. Expect to pay $18 a day for parking.

The **Hampton Inn & Suites** (175 Peabody Pl., 901/260-4000, www.bealestreetsuites.hamptoninn.com, $199-320) is less than a block from Beale Street. The Hampton Inn has 144 standard rooms with high-speed Internet and standard hotel accommodations. The 30 suites ($250) have kitchens and separate living quarters. The entire hotel is nonsmoking. Add $17 per day for parking.

Hampton Inn & Suites

$100-150

The most affordable downtown accommodations are in chain hotels. One of the best choices is the **Sleep Inn at Court Square** (40 N. Front St., 901/522-9700, $119-299), with 124 simple but clean and well-maintained rooms. Guests have access to a small fitness room, free parking, and a free continental breakfast. For those with a bigger appetite, the excellent Blue Plate Café is just across the square. It's a five-block walk to Beale Street from Court Square, but the trolley runs right past the front door of the hotel. Parking will run you $12 each day.

Even closer to the action is the 71-room **Comfort Inn Downtown** (100 N. Front St., 901/526-0583, $150-184). This hotel is within easy walking distance of all the city-center attractions. Rooms aren't anything special, but the staff is often quite friendly; guests get free breakfast, Internet access, and indoor parking; and there's an outdoor pool. Ask for a room facing west, and you'll have a nice view of the Mississippi River. Parking is $10 a day.

$150-200

Near AutoZone Park and a lot of restaurants is **Doubletree Downtown Memphis** (185 Union Ave., 901/528-1800, $134-299). A 272-room hotel set in the restored Tennessee Hotel, the Doubletree maintains a touch of the old grandeur of the 1929 hotel from which it was crafted. Rooms are large, and there's an outdoor swimming pool and fitness room. Valet parking is $22 or more per night.

If you want to be in the middle of things but can't afford to stay at the swanky Peabody, consider the **Holiday Inn Select** (160 Union Ave., 901/525-5491, www.hisdowntownmemphis.com, $139-199). Located across the street from the Peabody and near AutoZone Park, this Holiday Inn routinely gets good reviews from travelers.

Over $200

★ **The Peabody Memphis** (149 Union Ave., 901/529-4000 or 800/732-2639, www.peabodymemphis.com, $219-2,500 for a presidential suite) is the city's signature hotel. Founded in 1869, the Peabody was the grand hotel of the South, and the hotel has preserved some of its traditional Southern charm. Tuxedoed bellhops greet you at the door, and all guests receive a complimentary shoeshine. Rooms are nicely appointed with plantation-style furniture, free wireless Internet, and in-room safes, as well as all the amenities typical of an upper-tier hotel. Several fine restaurants are located on the ground floor, including the lobby bar, which is the gathering place for the twice-daily red carpet march of the famous Peabody ducks.

One of Memphis's newer hotels is the **River Inn of Harbor Town** (50 Harbor Town Sq., 901/260-3333, www.riverinnmemphis.com, $257-625). A 28-room boutique hotel on Mud Island, the River Inn offers great river views and a unique location that is just minutes from downtown. Set in the mixed residential and commercial New Urban community of Harbor Town, the River Inn provides guests with super amenities like a fitness center, reading rooms, free wireless Internet, free parking, modern decor and furniture, two restaurants, a 1.5-mile walking trail, and spa. Even the most modest rooms have luxurious extras like 32-inch flat-screen televisions, chocolate truffle turndown service, and full gourmet breakfast at Currents, one of two restaurants on the property. The River Inn offers the best of both worlds—a relaxing and quiet getaway that is uniquely convenient to the center of Memphis.

The decor at the **Madison Hotel** (79 Madison Ave., 901/333-1200, www.madisonhotelmemphis.com, $200-2,500) is modern, with a touch of art deco. Guests enjoy every perk you can imagine, from valet parking to room service from one of the city's finest restaurants, Grill 83. The daily continental breakfast and afternoon happy hour are an opportunity to enjoy the view from the top floor of the old bank building that houses the hotel. The 110 rooms have wet bars, Internet access, and luxurious bathrooms.

It is hard to describe the **Big Cypress Lodge** (1 Bass Pro Dr., 800/225-6343, big-cypress.com, $225-1,475) without making is sound a little crazy. First of all, this 103-room hotel is inside a giant pyramid that houses a Bass Pro Shop retail store. Opulent rooms are designed to look like treehouses and duck-hunting cabins. Rooms overlook the cypress swamp filled with alligators and fish and the retail shopping of the Bass Pro Shop. But for all its quirkiness, this hotel, which opened in 2015, is a luxury resort, with all the associated amenities, including a spa and a bowling alley. Expect to pay a $20 resort fee plus $20 per day for parking.

MIDTOWN

Midtown hotels are cheaper than those in downtown. By car, they are convenient to city-center attractions as well as those in midtown itself.

The Madison Hotel is an art deco oasis.

There are a few budget hotels within trolley distance of downtown. The **Quality Inn** (42 S. Camilla St., 901/526-1050, $72) is about two blocks from the Madison Avenue trolley and has an unremarkable but free breakfast. The **Motel 6** (210 S. Pauline St., 901/528-0650, $50-72) is about three blocks from the trolley. These choices are certainly not ritzy, but they're acceptable and welcome a large number of budget travelers.

$100-150

The **Best Western Gen X Inn** (1177 Madison Ave., 901/692-9136, $100-200) straddles downtown and midtown Memphis. Located about two miles from the city center along the Madison Avenue trolley line, Gen Xers can get downtown on the trolley in about 15 minutes, with a little luck. The hotel, which has free parking and breakfast, is also accessible to the city's expansive medical center and the attractions around Overton Park. These rooms are standard hotel style, enhanced with bright colors, flat-panel plasma TVs, and a general aura of youthfulness. The whole hotel is nonsmoking, and guests enjoy a good continental breakfast and a special partnership with the downtown YMCA for gym use. This is a good choice for travelers who want to be near downtown but are on a budget, particularly those with a car. No pets are permitted here.

$150-200

The **Holiday Inn-University of Memphis** (3700 Central Ave., 901/678-8200, $132-165) is part of the university's hospitality school. All rooms are suites, with a wet bar and microwave, sitting room, and spacious bathrooms. The lobby contains an exhibit on Kemmons Wilson, the Memphis-born founder of Holiday Inn, who is credited with inventing the modern hotel industry. It is located about six miles from downtown Memphis.

Over $200

The five rooms available in **The James Lee House** (690 Adams Ave, james-leehouse.com, 901/359-6750, $245-450) may be in one of the most opulent homes you've had the pleasure to stay in. The building may have been built in the 19th century, but the inn's amenities, such as wireless Internet and private gated parking, are 21st century.

You can sleep where Elvis slept at ★ **Lauderdale Courts** (252 N. Lauderdale St., 901/523-8662, $250). The onetime housing project where Elvis and his parents lived after they moved to Memphis from Mississippi is now a neat midtown apartment complex. The rooms where the Presleys lived have been restored to their 1950s greatness, and guests can use the working 1951 Frigidaire. The rooms are decorated with Presley family photographs and other Elvis memorabilia. You can rent Lauderdale Courts No. 328 for up to six nights. It sleeps up to four adults. The rooms are not rented during Elvis Week in August or his birthday week in January, when the suite is open for public viewing for $10 per person.

ACCOMMODATIONS

SOUTH MEMPHIS

There are two reasons to stay in south Memphis: the airport and Graceland. But even if you are keenly interested in either of these places, you should think twice about staying in this part of town. You will need a car, as some of these neighborhoods are seedy and south Memphis is not within walking distance of anything of interest.

Under $100

If you need to be close to the airport, the **Holiday Inn Memphis Airport Hotel & Conference Center** (2240 Democrat Rd., 901/332-1130, $100-160), which caters to business travelers, gets points for location, if not much else. There is a guest laundry, free airport shuttle, room service, a business center, and a decent fitness room.

You can't sleep much closer to Graceland than the **Days Inn at Graceland** (3839 Elvis Presley Blvd., 901/346-5500, $55-110), one of the most well-worn properties in the venerable Days Inn chain. The hotel has amped up the Elvis kitsch; you can tune into free nonstop Elvis movies or swim in a guitar-shaped pool. There is a free continental breakfast. Book early for Elvis Week.

The renovated **Kings Signature Hotel Airport/Graceland** (1471 E. Brooks Rd., 901/332-3500, www.cedarstreethospitality.com/thecedarhotel.php, $54-80) is a tidy, safe oasis in an otherwise unappealing part of town. Before its remodel, being close to Graceland and the airport were the only draws of this budget hotel. It remains affordable, but now it has the added perk of being clean, with updated rooms and bathrooms, plus a new restaurant and bar. There's a nice outdoor pool, a small fitness room, and a lovely lobby. Book early for Elvis Week.

$100-150

For the most Elvis-y Graceland digs, why not give in and stay at the **Elvis Presley Heartbreak Hotel** (3677 Elvis Presley Blvd., 901/332-1000, www.heartbreakhotel.net, $115-155)? This 128-room hotel has special Elvis-themed suites ($555-605), and the lobby and common areas have a special Elvis flair. Elvis enthusiasts should check out special package deals with the hotel and Graceland.

CAMPING

You can pitch your tent or park your RV just a 15-minute drive from downtown Memphis at **T. O. Fuller State Park** (1500 Mitchell Rd., 901/543-7581, tnstateparks.itinio.com/t-o-fuller, $20). The park has 45 tent and RV sites, each with a picnic table, fire ring, grill, lantern hanger, and electrical and water hookups.

On the north side of Memphis, **Meeman-Shelby Forest State Park** (910 Riddick Rd., Millington, 901/876-5215, $20) is a half-hour drive from downtown. Stay in one of six lakeside cabins, which you can reserve up to one year in advance; book at least one month in advance to avoid being shut out. The two-bedroom cabins can sleep up to six people. Rates are $85-100 per night, depending on the season and day of the week. There are also 49 tent/RV sites, each with electrical and water hookups, picnic tables, grills, and fire rings. The bathhouse has hot showers.

Food

Eating may be the best thing about visiting Memphis. The city's culinary specialties start—but don't end—with barbecue. Plate-lunch diners around the city offer delectable corn bread, fried chicken, greens, fried green tomatoes, peach cobbler, and dozens of other Southern specialties on a daily basis. And to make it even better, such down-home restaurants are easy on your wallet. For those seeking a departure from home-style fare, Memphis has dozens of fine restaurants, some old established eateries and others newcomers that are as trendy as those in any major American city.

Not sure where to start? Try a **Tastin' 'Round Town** food tour (901/310-9789, tastinroundtown.com). Choose from barbecue for $65 or Taste of Memphis for $48. These walking tours are multi-restaurant experiences that let you sample some of the city's best.

Memphis also has a decent food truck scene. Find one of the 45 trucks out and about (memphisfoodtruckers.org).

CAFÉS AND DINERS
Downtown

You can order deli sandwiches, breakfast plates, and a limited variety of plate lunches at the **Front Street Deli** (77 S. Front St., 901/522-8943, 7am-3pm Mon.-Fri., 8am-3pm Sat., $4-9, frontstreetdelicatessen.com). The deli, which claims to be Memphis's oldest, serves breakfast and lunch on weekdays only. One of its claims to fame is that scenes from *The Firm* were filmed here.

For the best burgers on Beale Street, go to **Dyer's** (205 Beale St., 901/527-3937, www.dyersonbeale.com, 11am-1am Sun.-Thurs., 11am-5am Fri.-Sat., $7-12). The legend is that Dyer's Burgers' secret is that it has been using the same grease (strained daily) since it opened in 1912. Only in Tennessee could century-old grease be a selling point. True or not, the burgers here are especially juicy. Dyer's also serves wings, hot dogs, milk shakes, and a full array of fried sides.

For coffee, pastries, and fruit smoothies, **Bluff City Coffee** (505 S. Main St., 901/405-4399, www.bluffcitycoffee.com, 6:30am-6pm Mon.-Sat., 8am-6pm Sun., $2-7.50) is your best bet in this part of the city. Located in the South Main district of galleries and condos, the shop is decorated with large prints of vintage Memphis photographs, and it is also a wireless Internet hot spot.

No restaurant has a larger or more loyal following in midtown than **Young Avenue Deli** (2119 Young Ave., 901/278-0034, www.youngavenuedeli.com, 11am-3am Mon.-Sat., noon-3am Sun., $4-8), which serves a dozen different specialty sandwiches, grill fare, including burgers and chicken sandwiches, plus salads and sides. The Bren—smoked turkey, mushrooms, onions, and cream cheese in a steamed pita—is a deli favorite. The food is certainly good, but it's the atmosphere at this homey yet hip Cooper-Young institution that really pulls in the crowds. There is live music most weekends, and the bar serves a kaleidoscope of domestic and imported beer, including lots of hard-to-find microbrews. The deli serves lunch and dinner daily.

For a good cup of coffee in the Cooper-Young neighborhood, head to **Java Cabana** (2170 Young Ave., 901/272-7210, www.javacabanacoffeehouse. com, 6:30am-10pm Tues.-Thurs., 9am-midnight Fri.-Sat., noon-10pm Sun., $4-7). Java Cabana serves light breakfast fare, including pancakes and omelets, all day. For lunch or later, you can order simple sandwiches or munchies like apple slices and peanut butter, potato chips, or Pop-Tarts.

Coffee shop and general store **City & State** (2625 Broad Ave., 901/249-2406, cityandstate.us, 7am-6pm Mon.-Fri., 8am-6pm Sat., 8am-2pm Sun., $1.50-9) peddles tea, coffee, pastries and sandwiches alongside locally made goods for retail sale, right in the heart of the Broad Avenue Arts District. Note: Credit cards only, no cash.

Chef Kelly English runs **The Second Line** (2144 Monroe Ave., 901/590-2829, secondlinememphis.com, 5pm-10pm Mon.-Thurs., 5pm-11pm Fri.,11am-11pm Sat., 11am-10pm Sun., $15-18). The kitchen rolls out New Orleans-inspired classics such as fried oyster po'boys and barbecue shrimp alongside southern dishes with a global twist, like roasted beet and feta shawarma or oyster rangoon.

the outdoor seating at Young Avenue Deli

Porcellino's Craft Butcher (711 W. Brookhaven Circle, 901/762-6656, porcellinoscraftbutcher.com, 7am-9pm Tues.-Sat., $10-28) is first and foremost a butcher shop selling cuts from local farms. It also doubles as a coffee shop in the morning and a sandwich shop come lunchtime, serving meaty options such as roast beef with giardiniera and horseradish aioli on a hoagie. When the sun sets, the space morphs into a cocktail bar serving small plates and heartier entrees centered around fresh cuts from the butcher case.

SOUTHERN
Downtown

Tucked inside an unassuming storefront across from the valet entrance to the Peabody Hotel is **Flying Fish** (105 S. 2nd St., 901/522-8228, 11am-10pm daily, $8-20), your first stop for authentic fried catfish in Memphis. If catfish isn't your thing, try the grilled or boiled shrimp, fish tacos, frog legs, or oysters. The baskets of fried seafood come with fries and hush puppies, and the grilled plates come with grilled veggies, rice, and beans. The tangy coleslaw is a must. The atmosphere here is laid-back; place your order at the window and come and get it when the coaster they give you starts to vibrate. The checkered tables are well stocked with hot sauce and saltines.

It would be a grave mistake to visit Memphis and not stop at ★ **Gus's World Famous Fried Chicken** (310 Front St., 901/527-4877, 11am-9pm Mon.-Thurs. and Sun., 11am-10:30pm Fri.-Sat., $6-12) for some of their delicious fried bird. The downtown location is a franchise of the original Gus's, which is a half-hour drive northeast out of town along U.S. 70, in Mason. It is no exaggeration to say that Gus's cooks up some of the best fried chicken out there: It is spicy, juicy, and hot. It's served casually wrapped in brown paper. Sides include coleslaw, baked beans, and fried pickles. The restaurant also serves grilled-cheese sandwiches. The service in this hole-in-the-wall establishment is slow but friendly, so come in with a smile on.

The **Arcade** (540 S. Main St., 901/526-5757, www.arcaderestaurant.com, 7am-3pm daily, $5-10) is said to be Memphis's oldest restaurant. Founded in 1919 and still operated by the same family (with lots of the same decor), this restaurant feels like a throwback to an earlier time. The menu is diverse, with pizzas, sandwiches, and plate-lunch specials during the week, and breakfast served anytime. The chicken spaghetti is a stick-to-your-ribs favorite.

Uptown

★ **The Little Tea Shop** (69 Monroe, 901/525-6000, 11am-2pm Mon.-Fri., $4.95-7.50) serves traditional plate lunches through the week. Choose from daily specials like fried catfish, chicken potpie, and meat loaf with your choice of vegetable and side dishes by ticking off boxes on the menu. Every meal (except sandwiches) comes with fresh, hot corn bread that might as well be the star of the show. This is stick-to-your-ribs Southern cooking at its best, so come hungry. If you have room, try the peach cobbler or pecan

FOOD

ball for dessert. The staff's welcoming yet efficient style makes this perfect for a quick lunch. Not to be missed.

The **Blue Plate Café** (113 Court Square S., 901/523-2050, 8am-2pm daily, $4-10) serves hearty breakfasts, plate lunches, and traditional home-style cooking. Its newsprint menu imparts wisdom ("Rule of Life No. 1: Wake up. Show up. Pay attention.") and declares that every day should begin with a great breakfast. It's not hard to comply at the Blue Plate. Eggs come with homemade biscuits and gravy, and your choice of grits, hash browns, or pancakes. For lunch, try a meat-and-three or vegetable plate, slow-cooked white-bean soup, or a grilled peanut butter and banana sandwich. Locals swear by the fried green tomatoes. There is also a Blue Plate Café in an old house in midtown (5469 Poplar Ave., 901/761-9696).

Alcenia's (317 N. Main St., 901/523-0200, www.alcenias.com, 11am-5pm Tues.-Fri., 9am-3pm Sat. , $9-11), located in the Pinch District, is among Memphis's best Southern-style restaurants. Known for its plate lunches, fried chicken, and pastries, Alcenia's has a style unlike any other Memphis eatery, witnessed in its offbeat decor of '60s-style beads, folk art, and wedding lace. Proprietor B. J. Chester-Tamayo is all love, and she pours her devotion into some of the city's best soul food. Try the spicy cabbage and deep-fried chicken, or the salmon croquette, and save room for Alcenia's famous bread pudding for dessert. Chicken and waffles is the Saturday morning specialty.

Midtown

Just follow the crowds to the **Cupboard Restaurant** (1400 Union Ave., 901/276-8015, www.thecupboardrestaurant.com, 7am-8pm daily, $6-10), one of Memphians' favorite stops for plate lunches. The Cupboard moved from its downtown location to an old Shoney's about a mile outside of town to accommodate the throngs who stop here for authentic home-style cooking. The Cupboard gets only the freshest vegetables for its dishes like okra and tomatoes, rutabaga turnips, steamed cabbage, and green beans. The meat specials change daily but include things like fried chicken, chicken and dumplings, hamburger steak with onions, and beef tips with noodles. The corn bread "coins" are exceptionally buttery, and the bread is baked fresh daily. For dessert, try the lemon icebox pie.

The Women's Exchange Tea Room (88 Racine St., 901/327-5681, www.womans-exchange.com, 11:30am-1:45pm Mon.-Fri., $8-15) feels like a throwback to an earlier era. Located one block east of the Poplar Street viaduct, the Women's Exchange has been serving lunch since 1936, and the menu has not changed much over the years. The special changes daily and always includes a choice of two entrées, or a four-vegetable plate. Classics like chicken salad, salmon loaf, beef tenderloin, and seafood gumbo are favorites, and all lunches come with a drink and dessert. The dining room looks out onto a green garden, and the atmosphere is homey—not stuffy. The Exchange also sells gifts, housewares, and other knickknacks.

In the Cooper-Young neighborhood, **Soul Fish** (862 S. Cooper St.,

901/725-0722, www.soulfishcafe.com, 11am-10pm Mon.-Sat., 11am-9pm Sun., $8-16) offers traditional plate lunches, vegetable plates, and several varieties of catfish. You can get the fish breaded and fried or blackened with a potent spice mix. Soul Fish is owned in part by Tiger Bryant, owner of the venerable Young Avenue Deli, and it has the hallmarks of a well-conceived eatery. The atmosphere is open and cheerful, with a few touches of subtle sophistication. In this case, the main attraction is good food at a good price—a combination that can be hard to find elsewhere in Cooper-Young. Soul Fish also has locations in East Memphis and Germantown.

FOOD

South Memphis

Gay Hawk Restaurant (685 Danny Thomas Blvd., 901/947-1464, 11am-3pm Mon.-Fri., noon-5pm Sun., $6-10) serves country-style food that sticks to your ribs and warms your soul. Chef Lewis Bobo declares that his specialty is "home-cooked food," and it really is as simple as that. The best thing about Gay Hawk is the luncheon buffet, which lets newcomers to Southern cooking survey the choices and try a little bit of everything. The Sunday lunch buffet practically sags with specialties like fried chicken, grilled fish, macaroni and cheese, greens, and much, much more. Save room for peach cobbler.

★ BARBECUE

Barbecue is serious business in Memphis, unlike anywhere else in the state. On the northern fringe of downtown Memphis is one of the city's most famous and well-loved barbecue joints: ★ **Cozy Corner** (745 N. Parkway, 901/527-9158, www.cozycornerbbq.com, 11am-9pm Tues.-Sat., $9-20). Cozy Corner is tucked into a storefront in an otherwise abandoned strip mall; you'll smell it before you see it. Step inside to order barbecue pork, sausage, or bologna sandwiches. Or get a two-bone, four-bone, or six-bone rib dinner plate, which comes with your choice of baked beans, coleslaw, or barbecue spaghetti, plus slices of Wonder bread to sop up the juices. One of Cozy Corner's specialties is its barbecued Cornish hens—a preparation that is surprising but delicious. Sweet tea goes perfectly with the tangy and spicy barbecue.

Jim Neely's **Interstate Bar-B-Que** (2265 S. 3rd St., 901/775-2304, www.interstatebarbecue.com, 11am-10pm Mon.-Wed., 11am-11pm Thurs., 11am-midnight Fri.-Sat., 11am-7pm Sun., $5-23) was once ranked the second-best barbecue in the nation, but the proprietors have not let it go to their heads; this is still a down-to-earth, no-frills eatery. Large appetites can order a whole slab of pork or beef ribs, but most people will be satisfied with a chopped pork sandwich, which comes topped with coleslaw and smothered with barbecue sauce. Families can get the fixings for 6, 8, or 10 sandwiches sent out family style. For an adventure, try the barbecue spaghetti or barbecue bologna sandwich. If you're in a hurry, Interstate has a drive-up window, too, and if you are really smitten, you can order pork, sauce, and seasoning in bulk to be frozen and shipped to your home.

Although aficionados will remind you that the ribs served at the **Rendezvous** (52 S. 2nd St., 901/523-2746, www.hogsfly.com, 4:30pm-10:30pm Tues.-Thurs., 11am-11pm Fri., 11:30am-11pm Sat., $8-20) are not technically barbecue, they are one of the biggest barbecue stories in town. Covered in a dry rub of spices and broiled until the meat falls off the bones, these ribs will knock your socks off. If you prefer, you can choose Charlie Vergos's dry-rub chicken or boneless pork loin. Orders come with baked beans and coleslaw, but beer is really the essential accompaniment to any Vergos meal. The door to Rendezvous is tucked in an alley off Monroe Avenue. The smoky interior, decorated with antiques and yellowing business cards, is low-key, noisy, and lots of fun.

Central BBQ (2249 Central, 901-272-9377, cbqmemphis.com, 11am-9pm daily, $5-25) appeals to both those who love dry rub and those who want their sauces. Can't decide between the pulled pork, the brisket, and other local favorites? Easy solution: Get the combo platter. Central has several locations around town.

A Memphis chain, **Gridley's** (6842 Stage Rd., 901/377-8055, 11am-8pm Sun., Mon., Wed., Thurs., 11am-9pm Fri.-Sat., $4-18) serves wet-style barbecue ribs, pork shoulder plates and sandwiches, plus spicy grilled shrimp. The shrimp is served with a buttery and delicious dipping sauce. Try the half-pork, half-shrimp plate for a real treat. Meals here come with baked beans, slaw, and hot, fresh bread. Sometimes Gridley's closes on Wednesdays, so call ahead if you are headed there on hump day.

The mustard slaw at **Leonard's Pit Barbecue** (5465 Fox Plaza Dr., 901/360-1963, www.leonardsbarbecue.com, 11am-2:30pm Sun.-Thurs., 11am-9pm Fri.-Sat., $5-20) is an essential side dish to complement the classic Memphis barbecue.

CONTEMPORARY
Downtown

The Majestic Grille (145 S. Main St., 901/522-8555, www.majesticgrille. com, 11am-10pm Mon.-Thurs., 11am-11pm Fri., 11am-2:30pm and 4pm-11pm Sat., 11am-2:30pm and 4pm-9pm Sun., $8-48) serves a remarkably affordable yet upscale menu at brunch, lunch, and dinner. Located in what was once the Majestic Theater, the restaurant's white tablecloths and apron-clad waiters lend an aura of refinement. But with main courses starting at just $8-9, this can be a bargain. Flatbread pizzas feature asparagus, spicy shrimp, and smoked sausage, and sandwiches include burgers and clubs. Specialties include pasta, barbecue ribs, grilled salmon, and steaks. Don't pass on dessert, served in individual shot glasses, such as chocolate mousse, key lime pie, and carrot cake, among others.

It is impossible to pigeonhole **Automatic Slim's Tonga Club** (83 S. 2nd St., 901/525-7948, automaticslimsmemphis.com, 11 am-11 pm Mon.-Thurs., 11 am-1am Fri., 9 am-1am Sat., 9am-11pm Sun., brunch $8-14, lunch $9-14, dinner $16-27), except to say that this Memphis institution consistently offers fresh, spirited, and original fare. Named after a character from an old blues tune, Automatic Slim's uses lots of strong flavors to create its eclectic menu; Caribbean and Southwestern influences are the most apparent. Take a seat and in two shakes you'll be presented with soft, fresh bread and pesto-seasoned olive oil for dipping. Start with Lobster Tater Tots or Coconut Shrimp, or come for brunch and an Oreo Waffle. A meal at Automatic Slim's would not be complete without a famous Tonga Martini or one of the kitchen's delectable desserts: Pecan tart and chocolate cake are good choices. Automatic Slim's is a welcome departure from barbecue and Southern food when you're ready. Its atmosphere is relaxed, and there's often a crowd at the bar, especially on weekends, when there's live music on tap.

Long the standard-bearer of fine French cuisine, **Chez Philippe** (149 Union Ave., 901/529-4188, 6pm-10pm Wed.-Sat., $78-100, three-course afternoon tea 1pm-3:30pm Wed.-Sat., $30-40/$24 kids), located in the Peabody Hotel, now offers French-Asian fusion cuisine. The Asian influences are noticeable in the ingredients, but the preparation of most dishes at Chez Philippe remains traditional French. Entrées include grouper, bass, pork chop, and venison. Chez Philippe offers a prix fixe menu: Three-course meals are $80 and five courses, $105.

Midtown

In 2007, Memphis's foremost restaurateur, Karen Blockman Carrier, closed her fine-dining restaurant Cielo in Victorian Village, redecorated, and reopened it as the **Molly Fontaine Lounge** (679 Adams Ave., 901/524-1886, molliefontainelounge.com, 5 p.m.-"'til the spirits go to sleep" Wed.-Sat., $8-11). Carrier's vision was an old-fashioned club where guests can order upscale cocktails, relax with live music, and eat tasty Mediterranean- and Middle Eastern-inspired tapas. The restaurant has an upmarket but cozy atmosphere, with equal measures of funky and fine. The live piano jazz is the perfect backdrop for the restaurant's artistic small plates.

Surprisingly good for a bookstore café, **The Booksellers Bistro** (387 Perkins Ext., 901/374-0881, thebooksellersatlaurelwood.com/bronte-bistro, 8am-9pm Mon.-Thurs., 8am-10pm Fri.-Sat., 9am-8pm Sun., $10-17), offers salads, soups, and sandwiches, as well as daily meat and fish specials. The soup-and-sandwich combo is filling and good. Breakfast may well be the best meal on offer, however. The morning menu features specials designed by celebrity chefs, including omelets, baked goods, and crepes.

One of Memphis's most distinctive restaurant settings is an old beauty shop in the Cooper-Young neighborhood. ★ **The Beauty Shop** (966 S. Cooper St., 901/272-7111, www.thebeautyshoprestaurant.com, 11am-2pm Mon.-Sat. and 5pm-10pm Mon.-Thurs., 5pm-11pm Fri.-Sat., 10am-3pm Sun., lunch $6.50-10, dinner entrées $23-26) takes advantage of the vintage beauty parlor decor to create a great talking point for patrons and food writers alike. The domed hair dryers remain, and the restaurant has put the shampooing sinks to work as beer coolers. At lunch, the Beauty Shop offers a casual menu of sandwiches and salads. For dinner, the imaginative cuisine

of Memphis restaurateur Karen Blockman Carrier, who also owns Molly
Fontaine Lounge and Automatic Slim's Tonga Club, takes over.

If you enjoy your beer as much or more than your meal, then head
straight for **Boscos Squared** (2120 Madison Ave., 901/432-2222, www.
boscosbeer.com, 11am-2am Mon.-Thurs., 11am-3am Fri.-Sat., 10:30am-
2am Sun., lunch $10-15, dinner $11-24). Boscos is a brewpub with fresh
seafood, steak, and pizza. Its beer menu is among the best in the city, and
many of the brews are made on the premises.

Bolstering the craft butchery trend is **Bounty on Broad** (2519 Broad Ave.
901/410-8131, bountyonbroad.com, 5pm-9:30pm Tues.-Thurs., 5pm-10pm
Fri.-Sat., 11am-2pm. Sun., $14-25), a restaurant and boutique butcher shop.
On the restaurant side, expect family-style dishes with a farm-to-table slant.
Note: Cash is not accepted, just credit cards.

East Memphis

To many minds, Memphis dining gets no better than ★ **Erling Jensen,
The Restaurant** (1044 S. Yates Rd., 901/763-3700, www.ejensen.com, 5pm-
10pm daily, $33-50). Danish-born Erling Jensen is the mastermind of this
fine-dining restaurant that has consistently earned marks as Memphians'
favorite restaurant. Understated decor and friendly service are the backdrop to Jensen's dishes, which are works of art. The menu changes with
the seasons and is based upon availability, but usually it includes about
six different seafood dishes and as many meat and game choices. Black
Angus beef, elk loin, and buffalo tenderloin are some of the favorites. Meals
at Jensen's restaurant should begin with an appetizer, salad, or soup—or
all three. The jumbo chunk crab cakes with smoked red-pepper sauce are
excellent. Reservations are a good idea at Erling Jensen, and so are jackets
for men. Expect to spend upwards of $80 for a four-course meal here; $60
for two courses. Add more for wine.

Memphis's premier steak house is **Folk's Folly** (551 S. Mendenhall Rd.,
901/762-8200, www.folksfolly.com, 5:30pm-10pm Mon.-Sat., 5:30pm-
9pm Sun., $35-70), located just east of Audubon Park. Diners flock here
for prime aged steaks and seafood favorites. For small appetites, try the
8-ounce filet mignon for $32; large appetites can gorge on the 28-ounce
porterhouse for $65. Seafood includes lobster, crab legs, and wild salmon.
The atmosphere is classic steak house: The lighting is low, and there's a
piano bar on the property.

Some say **Acre Restaurant** (690 S. Perkins, 901/818-2273, www.acre-
memphis.com, lunch: 11am-2pm Mon.-Fri., dinner: 5pm-10pm Mon.-
Sat., $22-35) is Memphis's best. Certainly, it has one of the best wine lists
in town. The menu combines southern and Asian traditions with locally
grown and raised ingredients in a modern setting.

Where else in the world can you enjoy the offbeat combination that is
Jerry's Sno-Cone and Car Wash (1657 Wells Station Rd., 901/767-2659,
11am-7pm Mon.-Sat.)? Choose from more than 70 varieties of shaved ice.

Piggly Wiggly

Memphian Clarence Saunders opened the first **Piggly Wiggly** at 79 Jefferson Street in 1916, thus giving birth to the modern American supermarket. Until then, shoppers went to small storefront shops where they would ask the counter clerk for what they needed: a pound of flour, a half-dozen pickles, a block of cheese. The clerk went to the bulk storage area at the rear of the store and measured out what the customer needed.

Saunders's big idea was self-service. At the Piggly Wiggly, customers entered the store, carried a basket, and were able to pick out prepackaged and priced containers of food that they paid for at the payment station on their way out.

Suffice to say, the Piggly Wiggly idea took off, and by 1923 there were 1,268 Piggly Wiggly franchises around the country. Saunders used some of his profits to build a massive mansion east of the city out of pink Georgia limestone, but he was never to live in the Pink Palace, which he lost as a result of a complex stock loss.

Today, **Saunders's Pink Palace** is home to the **Pink Palace Museum,** which includes, among other things, a replica of the original Piggly Wiggly supermarket.

FOOD

INTERNATIONAL
Downtown

For sushi, try **Sekisui** (Union at 2nd Ave., 901/523-0001, www.sekisuiusa.com, noon-3pm and 6pm-11pm daily, where a roll costs $2.50-8, and a filling combo plate will run you about $15). Sekisui is a Memphis chain, and there are other locations in midtown (25 S. Belvedere Blvd., 901/725-0005, 11:30am-2pm and 5pm-9:30pm Mon.-Thurs., 11:30am-2pm and 5pm-10:30pm Fri., 5pm-10:30pm Sat., 5pm-9:30pm Sun.).

Lively, funky **Oshi Burger Bar** (94 S. Main St., 901/341-2091, oshiburger.com, 11am-10pm Sun.-Thurs., 11am-midnight Fri.-Sat., $7-12) specializes in burgers and hot dogs with an Asian twist: think toppings such as kimchi slaw or nori flakes and sides such as tempura onion rings. Milkshakes with additions like Pop Rocks, sake, bacon dust, or bourbon are a fun treat.

Midtown

The **India Palace** (1720 Poplar Ave., 901/278-1199, www.indiapalaceinc.com, lunch: 11am-3pm Mon.-Fri., dinner: 5pm-9:30pm Mon.-Thurs., 5pm-10pm Fri.-Sun., $9-17) is a regular winner in readers' choice polls for Indian food in Memphis. The lunchtime buffet is filling and economical, and the dinner menu features vegetarian, chicken, and seafood dishes. The dinner platters are generous and tasty.

Pho Hoa Binh (1615 Madison, 901/276-0006, 11am-9pm Mon.-Fri., noon-9pm Sat., $4-9) is one of the most popular Vietnamese restaurants in town. You can't beat the value of the lunch buffet, or you can order from the dizzying array of Chinese and Vietnamese dishes, including spring rolls, vermicelli noodle bowls, rice, and meat dishes. There are a lot of vegetarian options here.

The atmosphere at **Bhan Thai** (1324 Peabody Ave., 901/272-1538, www. bhanthairestaurant.com, 11am-2:30pm Tues.-Fri., 5pm-9:30pm Sun.-Thurs., 5pm-10:30pm Fri.-Sat., $14-23) in midtown is almost as appealing as the excellent Thai food served there. Set in an elegant 1912 home, Bhan Thai makes the most of the house's space, and seating is spread throughout several colorful rooms and on the back patio. Choose from dishes like red snapper, masaman curry, and roasted duck curry. The Bhan Thai salad is popular, with creamy peanut dressing and crisp vegetables.

It's the regulars who are happy at the **Happy Mexican Restaurant and Cantina** (385 S. 2nd St., 901/529-9991, www.happymexican.com, 11am-10pm Sun.-Thurs., 11am-11pm Fri.-Sat., $7-15). Serving generous portions of homemade Mexican food for lunch and dinner, Happy Mexican is destined to become a downtown favorite. The service is efficient and friendly, and the decor is cheerful but not over the top. It's located just a few blocks south of the National Civil Rights Museum. There are three other locations in the greater Memphis area.

Ecco on Overton Park (1585 Overton Park, 901/410-8200, eccoonover-tonpark.com, 11am-2pm and 4:30pm-9pm Tues.-Thurs., 11am-2pm and 5:30pm-9:30pm Fri., 10am-2pm and 5:30pm-9:30pm Sat., $12-28) channels all the comforts of a European café with dishes such as cassoulet, pasta puttanesca and burgundy-sauced beef short ribs. Drink as the Italians do with an Aperol spritz or sip a bit of Spain with a bottle of rosé from Rioja.

Robata Ramen & Yakitori Bar (2116 Madison Ave. 901/410-8290, ro-batamemphis.com, 5pm-midnight daily, $7-15) is equal parts fun and af-fordable, with an array of yakitori (bite-size meats and veggies that are skewered, then grilled) sold by the piece and a create-your-own ramen menu.

East Memphis

Andrew Michael Italian Kitchen (712 W. Brookhaven Circle, 901/347-3569, andrewmichaelitaliankitchen.com, 5pm-10pm Tues.-Sat., $10-30) is home to chefs Andrew Ticer and Michael Hudman—who were honored as finalists in the Best Chef: Southeast category for the 2015 James Beard Foundation Awards. They learned the nuances of Italian cooking from their grandmothers as well as travels throughout Italy. Ticer and Hudman also own Porcellino's.

VEGETARIAN
Midtown

Raw and vegan food delivery service **Raw Girls Memphis** (raw-girls-mem-phis.myshopify.com) also runs two food trucks that dole out cold-pressed juices, snacks, soups, salads and sandwiches. Eats are as clean as it gets—free of gluten, dairy, and refined sugar, a boon for those navigating food allergies or sensitivities—featuring organic, locally grown produce to boot.

Look for the trucks parked in Midtown (242 S. Cooper, 10am-6pm Wed.-Sun., $7-9) and East Memphis (5502 Poplar Ave., same hours).

MARKETS

The closest gourmet grocery is located in Harbor Town, the residential community on Mud Island, where **Miss Cordelia's** (737 Harbor Bend, 901/526-4772, www.misscordelias.com, 7am-10pm daily) sells fresh produce, bakery goods, and staples. A deli in the back serves soups, salads, sandwiches, and a wide variety of prepared foods.

For a full-service grocery store in midtown, look for the **Kroger** at the corner of Cleveland and Poplar.

The **Memphis Farmers Market** (901/575-0580, www.memphisfarmersmarket.com, Sat. 7am-1pm Apr.-Oct., rain or shine) takes place in the pavilion opposite Central Station in the South Main part of town.

For liquor and wine, go to **The Corkscrew** (511 S. Front St., 901/523-9389, www.corkscrewmemphis.com, 10am-11pm Mon.-Sat.).

Information and Services

INFORMATION
Visitors Centers

The city's visitors center is the **Tennessee Welcome Center** (119 Riverside Dr., 901/543-6757), located on the Tennessee side of the I-40 bridge. The center has lots of brochures and free maps and staff who can answer your questions. It is open 24 hours a day, seven days a week. The center assists more than 350,000 travelers annually.

Although it is not designed to be a visitors center per se, the **Memphis Convention and Visitors Bureau** (47 Union Ave., 901/543-5300, www.memphistravel.com, 8:30am-5pm Mon.-Thurs., 8:30am-4pm Fri.) is a resource for visitors. You can collect maps and ask questions here. The bureau also produces videos highlighting city attractions and restaurants, which are available on many hotel televisions. Other locations are on Riverside Drive and State Route 385 at I-40.

Hand-out maps that highlight key attractions are available from visitors centers in Memphis. If you are only interested in Beale Street, Graceland, and the interstates, these will be fine. The free maps provided at the concierge desk of the Peabody Hotel are particularly well marked and useful.

If you want to explore further, or if you plan to drive yourself around the city, it is wise to get a proper city map or GPS. Rand McNally publishes a detailed Memphis city map, which you can buy from bookstores or convenience marts in downtown.

Media

The daily *Commercial Appeal* (www.commercialappeal.com) is Memphis's major newspaper, available all over the city. The *Memphis Flyer* (www.

memphisflyer.com) is a free alternative weekly, published on Wednesday, with the best entertainment listings.

Memphis magazine (www.memphismagazine.com) is published monthly and includes historical anecdotes, restaurant reviews, features on high-profile residents, and lots of advertising aimed at residents and would-be residents.

There are two independent radio stations of note: **WEVL 89.9 FM** is a community radio station that plays blues, country, and other Memphis music. **WDIA 1070 AM,** the historical Memphis station that made the blues famous, still rocks today. Another noteworthy station is **WRBO 103.5 FM,** which plays soul and R&B.

SERVICES
Fax and Internet
Send a fax at the **FedEx Office** (50 N. Front St., 901/521-0261), located across from the Peabody's valet entrance.

Most of the major hotels and attractions have wireless Internet access.

Postal Service
There is a postal retail center, which sells stamps and offers limited postal services, at 100 Peabody Place (800/275-8777, 8:30am-5pm Mon.-Fri.).

Emergency Services
Dial 911 in an emergency for fire, ambulance, or police. The downtown police department is the **South Main Station** (545 S. Main St., 901/636-4099). Police patrol downtown by car, on bike, and on foot.

Several agencies operate hotlines for those needing help. They include: Alcoholics Anonymous (901/726-6750), the Better Business Bureau (901/759-1300), Emergency Mental Health Services (855/274-7471), Deaf Interpreting (901/577-3783), Rape Crisis/Sexual Assault Hotline (901/272-2020), and Poison Emergencies (901/528-6048).

Hospitals
Memphis is chockablock with hospitals. Midtown Memphis is also referred to as Medical Center for the number of hospitals and medical facilities there. Here you will find the **Regional Medical Center at Memphis** (877 Jefferson Ave., 901/545-7100), a 325-bed teaching hospital affiliated with the University of Tennessee; and the **Methodist University Hospital** (1265 Union Ave., 901/516-7000), the 617-bed flagship hospital for Methodist Healthcare.

In East Memphis, **Baptist Memorial Hospital** (6019 Walnut Grove Rd., 901/226-5000) is the cornerstone of the huge Baptist Memorial Health Care System, with 771 beds.

Laundry

Try any of these two laundries, which are located near downtown: **Crump Laundry Mat and Dry Cleaning** (756 E. Ed Crump Blvd., 901/948-7008) or **Jackson Coin Laundry** (1216 Jackson Ave., 901/274-3536).

Libraries

Memphis has 18 public libraries. The city's main library is **Hooks Public Library** (3030 Poplar Ave., 901/415-2700, 10am-8pm Mon.-Thurs., 10am-5pm Fri.-Sat., 1pm-5pm Sun.), a modern, new public library with 119 public computers, an extensive book collection, community programs, meeting rooms, a lecture series, and more. The central library is located on a busy thoroughfare in midtown and would be a challenge to visit without a car.

The downtown branch library, **Cossit Library** (33 S. Front St., 901/415-2766, 10am-5pm Mon.-Fri.), has a good collection of new releases, and staff there are happy to help visitors looking for information about Memphis. The current building was constructed in 1959, but the Cossit Library was founded in 1888 as the Cossit-Goodwyn Institute.

Getting There and Around

GETTING THERE
Air

Memphis International Airport (MEM, 901/922-8000, www.mscaa.com) is located 13 miles south of downtown Memphis. There are two popular routes to Memphis from the airport. Take I-240 north to arrive in midtown. To reach downtown, take I-55 north and exit on Riverside Drive. The drive takes 20-30 minutes.

The airport's main international travel insurance and business services center (901/922-8090) is located in ticket lobby B and is open daily. Here you can exchange foreign currency, buy travel insurance, conduct money transfers, send faxes and make photocopies, and buy money orders and travelers checks. A smaller kiosk near the international arrivals and departures area at gate B-36 is open daily and offers foreign currency exchange and travel insurance.

There is wireless Internet service in the airport, but it is not free.

AIRPORT SHUTTLE

TennCo Express (901/645-3726, www.tenncoexpress.com) provides an hourly shuttle service from the airport to many downtown hotels. Tickets are $20 one-way and $30 round-trip. Look for the shuttle parked in the third lane near column number 14 outside the airport terminal. Shuttles depart every half hour 7:30am-9:30pm. For a hotel pickup, call at least a day in advance.

Car

Memphis is located at the intersection of two major interstate highways: I-40, which runs east-west across the United States, and I-55, which runs south from St. Louis to New Orleans.

Many people who visit Memphis drive here in their own cars. The city is 300 miles from St. Louis, 380 miles from Atlanta, 410 miles from New Orleans, 450 miles from Dallas, 480 miles from Cincinnati and Oklahoma City, and 560 miles from Chicago.

Bus

Greyhound (800/231-2222, www.greyhound.com) runs daily bus service to Memphis from around the United States. Direct service is available to Memphis from a number of surrounding cities, including Jackson and Nashville, Tennessee; Tupelo and Jackson, Mississippi; Little Rock and Jonesboro, Arkansas; and St. Louis. The Greyhound station (3033 Airways Blvd., 901/395-8770) is open 24 hours a day.

Train

Amtrak (800/872-7245, www.amtrak.com) runs the City of New Orleans train daily between Chicago and New Orleans, stopping in Memphis on the way. The southbound train arrives daily at Memphis's Central Station at 6:27am, leaving about half an hour later. The northbound train arrives at 10pm every day. It is an 11-hour ride overnight between Memphis and Chicago, and about 8 hours between Memphis and New Orleans.

The Amtrak station (901/526-0052) is located in Central Station at 545 South Main Street in the South Main district of downtown. Ticket and baggage service is available at the station daily 5:45am-11:15pm.

GETTING AROUND

Driving

Driving is the most popular and easiest way to get around Memphis. Downtown parking is plentiful if you are prepared to pay; an all-day pass in one of the many downtown parking garages costs about $12. Traffic congestion peaks, predictably at rush hours and is worst in the eastern parts of the city and along the interstates.

Public Transportation

BUSES

The **Memphis Area Transit Authority** (901/274-6282, www.matatransit. com) operates dozens of buses that travel through the greater Memphis area. For information on routes, call or stop by the North End Terminal on North Main Street for help planning your trip. The bus system is not used frequently by tourists. A daily pass is available for $3.50 or $16/week.

Public trolleys (or hybrid bus shuttles when the trolleys are being serviced) run for about two miles along Main Street in Memphis from the Pinch District in the north to Central Station in the south, and circle up on a parallel route along Riverfront Drive. Another trolley line runs about two miles east on Madison Avenue, connecting the city's medical center with downtown. The Main Street Trolleys run every 10 minutes at most times, but the Madison Avenue trolleys run less often on weekends and evenings after 6pm.

Fares are $1 per ride. You can buy an all-day pass for $3.50, a three-day pass for $9, or a monthlong pass for $25. All passes must be purchased at the North End Terminal at the northern end of the Main Street route.

The trolley system is useful, especially if your hotel is on either the northern or southern end of downtown or along Madison Avenue. Brochures with details on the routes and fares are available all over town, or you can download one at www.matatransit.com. The trolleys are simple to understand and use; if you have a question, just ask your driver.

SUN STUDIO FREE SHUTTLE BUS

Sun Studio runs a free shuttle between Sun Studio, the Rock 'n' Soul Museum at Beale Street, and Graceland. The first run stops at the Graceland Heartbreak Hotel at 9:55am, Graceland at 10am, Sun Studio at 10:15am, and the Rock 'n' Soul Museum at 10:30am. Runs continue throughout the day on an hourly schedule. The last run picks up at Heartbreak Hotel at 5:55pm, Graceland Plaza at 6pm, and Sun Studio at 6:15pm.

The shuttle is a 12-passenger black van painted with the Sun Studio logo. The ride is free, but consider tipping your driver. The published schedule is a loose approximation, so it's a good idea to get to the pickup point early in case the van is running ahead. You can call 901/521-0664 for more information.

Taxis

Memphis has a number of taxi companies, and you will usually find available cabs along Beale Street and waiting at the airport. Otherwise, you will need to call for a taxi. Some of the largest companies are **Yellow Cab** (901/577-7777), **City Wide Cab** (901/722-8294), **Arrow Transportation Company** (901/332-7769), and **Metro Cab** (901/322-2222, ridememphis. com). Expect to pay $25-35 for a trip from the airport to downtown; most fares around town are under $10. Taxis accept credit cards. App-based ride-sharing services like Uber and Lyft (approximately $17 from the airport to downtown) operate in Memphis and have agreements with the local government to allow them to make stops at the airport and other destinations.

GETTING THERE AND AROUND

Background

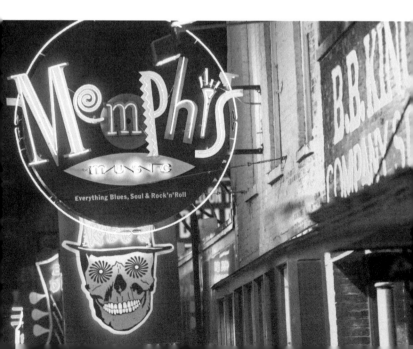

The Landscape

Tennessee is a long, narrow state. Shaped roughly like a parallelogram, it is 500 miles from east to west and 110 miles from north to south. Partly due to its unusual shape, Tennessee, along with Missouri, borders more states than any other in the country. Its neighbors are North Carolina, Virginia, Kentucky, Missouri, Arkansas, Mississippi, Alabama, and Georgia. Tennessee is the 36th-largest state in the United States, with a land mass of 41,234 square miles.

Like the rest of the United States, Tennessee was covered by a large shallow sea approximately 500 million years ago. As the sea dried up, the land that is now Tennessee turned swampy and eventually dry. The sea creatures that once lived in the sea died, their skeletons forming limestone. The plants and animals that lived in the swampy landscape died, eventually forming coal.

Beginning about 600 million years ago, the Appalachian Mountains were formed through plate movement. Once sharp and rocky, the Appalachians have been worn down over millions of years to the gentle, rounded slopes that now characterize the range.

GEOGRAPHY

If you ask a Tennessean where he is from, the answer is never as simple as "Tennessee." Tennessee is divided by the Tennessee River into three "Grand Divisions": East Tennessee, Middle Tennessee, and West Tennessee. These are even represented on the state flag and seal.

West Tennessee is more like the Deep South than the rest of the state. Mostly flat and rural, this was the epicenter of the state's cotton industry both before and after the Civil War. The Gulf Coastal Plain, an area of 9,000 square miles, is drained by the Mississippi River and its tributaries. Memphis lies in the southwestern corner of this area.

RIVERS AND LAKES

The largest river in Tennessee is the Mississippi River, which forms the western border of the state. The Hatchie River is among the smaller tributaries that drain West Tennessee and flow into the Mississippi.

The state's two most important rivers are the Cumberland and Tennessee Rivers. The Cumberland River flows through Nashville and along the north-central portion of the state. The Tennessee River flows in a *U* shape, first flowing south through East Tennessee, through Knoxville and Chattanooga, and then northward, defining the boundary between Middle and West Tennessee. Both the Cumberland and the Tennessee Rivers empty into the Ohio River, which flows to the Mississippi.

All but one of Tennessee's major lakes are artificial, having been created

Previous: dragon boat races on the Mississippi River; neon Memphis sign on Beale Street.

by the Tennessee Valley Authority (TVA) during the last century. The lone exception to this is Reelfoot Lake in northeastern Tennessee, which was formed from the 1811 New Madrid earthquake when the mouth of what had been Reelfoot Creek was closed off and the creek's water spread out to cover the surrounding land.

CLIMATE

Tennessee has a mild climate. The average temperature is 58°F; in winter, temperatures generally hover 30-40°F, and summer temperatures are 70-80°F. Summer days can feel very hot, however, particularly in Middle and West Tennessee. Memphis temperatures rise significantly during the summer, and the city stays warmest in winter. The state receives an average of 50 inches of rain per year.

Tornadoes

The Mid-South, including western and central Tennessee, is prone to tornadoes. The tornado season runs November-April, but can continue into the summer. The danger of tornadoes is compounded by the fact that they may strike after dark and that in many areas of the state, visibility is limited by hills and trees.

On Super Tuesday, February 5, 2008, a series of tornadoes struck Tennessee, killing 32 people, most of them in Sumner and Macon Counties north of Nashville. Of those who died, 20 were in mobile homes when the storm struck. The event, one of the most deadly natural disasters in Tennessee history, led to calls for better education and awareness.

The best way to avoid injury in a tornado is to monitor a weather radio and move quickly to a cellar, basement, or windowless interior room if a tornado is on the way.

Floods

The devastating flood in Nashville and Middle Tennessee in May 2010 brought the issue of global climate changes, combined with man-made development and water management, to the forefront of the minds of city planners and residents. The flood caused more than $1.5 billion of damage to the Music City, although it quickly rallied and rebuilt. Floods were also a concern in 2011 when the Mississippi threatened to cover parts of Memphis with water.

ENVIRONMENTAL ISSUES
Air Pollution

Car emissions, industrial pollution, and other activities cause air pollution. In Tennessee, exhaust from cars and trucks, plus the toxic emissions from coal-fired generating plants, are the biggest contributors to air pollution.

Water Pollution

The cleanliness of Tennessee's rivers, lakes, and streams is monitored according to the standards of the Clean Water Act. The Tennessee Department of Environment and Conservation monitors the health of the state's rivers. In its last report, the agency reported that 25 percent of the state's river miles were category one, the cleanest, and 31 percent were in the dirtiest category. As for lakes and reservoirs, 21 percent of lake acres were classified as "impaired."

Most water pollution is caused by sedimentation and silt runoff from construction and agriculture. Habitat alteration, pathogens found in wastewater, and nutrients from fertilizers are also problems. Some pollution can be readily cleaned up, but so-called legacy pollutants, such as PCBs (polychlorinated biphenyl) and chlordane from old industrial sites, can remain present for years and can poison fish and other marine animals.

According to the state government, 41 percent of pollution in streams and rivers in 2006 came from agriculture, 19 percent from hydrologic modification, and 18 percent from municipal sources. For lakes, 72 percent of contaminants were legacy pollutants.

The state is supposed to post a warning when a river or stream is deemed too polluted for fishing, swimming, or other forms of use. For a listing of such bodies of water, contact the Water Pollution Control division of the Department of Environment and Conservation (615/532-0625), or the Tennessee Clean Water Network (www.tcwn.org).

Plants and Animals

Encyclopedias are written about Tennessee's rich and diverse menagerie of animals and plants. Middle and West Tennessee share the more typical plants and animals of the Deep South. Western Tennessee's cypress swamps are rich depositories of plant and animal life, while the plains are important for agriculture.

WILDFLOWERS

In the spring and summer, wildflowers spring up along roadsides, mountain streams, and pastures. Look for the small yellow blooms of **St. John's wort** and the bushy purple crowns of **ironweed.** Delicate purple **bluebells** and white, pink, or purple **phlox** blanket cool stream banks and coves. Placid lakes and ponds come alive with the white-pink blooms of **water lily.**

Fields and gardens are decorated with the bracing yellow blooms of **sunflowers** and the bright-orange colors of **butterfly weed.** Cultivated lawns and gardens showcase delicate **roses** and elegant **irises,** the state flower of Tennessee.

TREES

Tennessee's official state tree is the **tulip poplar,** a fast-growing tree often used for timber. It blooms in May. Throughout the state you will see **magnolia** trees, notable for their thick, heavy green leaves and large white blooms, as well as their sweet scent.

In West Tennessee's wetlands and at Reelfoot Lake, look for **cypress** trees, easily identifiable by their rough, bumpy knees.

BIRDS

Field, swamp, house, chipping, and song **sparrows,** as they flit about and perch on tree limbs, are ubiquitous in the Volunteer State. Look for the red **cardinal,** the black-and-white **junco,** and the yellow **goldfinch.**

The **Carolina chickadee** puffs out its breast in winter, and the **blue jay** patrols bird feeders. The **mockingbird** is Tennessee's state bird; it mimics the calls of other birds and has a gray body and dark wings.

Unless you are unusually patient or light of foot, you're unlikely to see the nocturnal **Eastern screech owl** or its cousins, the great horned owl and barred owl, in the wild. Keep your eyes pinned on the sky for **hawks,** red-tailed, sharp-shinned, and Cooper's. **Bald eagles** winter at Reelfoot Lake and other protected locations in the state.

Wild turkeys are making a comeback; groups may be seen patrolling many state parks and natural areas. Look for the male's impressive feathers. Listen for the knocking of the **woodpeckers**—hairy, redheaded, downy, and pileated varieties.

Bodies of water are some of the best places to seek feathered friends. **Sandhill cranes** winter on the Hiwassee River in East Tennessee. Float down a river, and you may see a statuesque **great blue heron** hunting for food. **Wood ducks** and **mallards,** whose males have a striking green head, live around ponds and lakes.

SMALL MAMMALS

Raccoons, with their bandit's mask and striped tail, are adorable until one has ruined your bird feeder or gotten into your garbage (or even bitten you, which has been known to happen). **Eastern cottontail** is the most common type of rabbit, and they prefer grasslands and cultivated areas. Look for the white of their stubby tail. **Eastern chipmunks** are small creatures that scurry along forest floors, pastureland, and city parks. **Eastern gray squirrels** are easier to see—they are larger and more ubiquitous.

AMPHIBIANS AND REPTILES

Listen for the "harumph" of the **bullfrog** or the night song of the **Cope's gray tree frog** near water. Salamanders and newts flourish in the damp, cool forests of the eastern mountains: look for the lizard-like **Eastern newt** and the **spotted salamander,** which can grow up to 10 inches. The largest of the salamanders is the **Eastern tiger salamander,** which comes in a rainbow of colors and patterns best left to your imagination. They grow up to 13 inches.

Snapping turtles live in rivers and streams, rarely coming on land. The **Eastern box turtle** prefers moist forests and grasslands. Most Tennessee snakes are harmless. The **garter snake** is the most common. It prefers areas that are cool and moist. **Green snakes** like bushes and low-hanging branches near the water.

History

THE FIRST TENNESSEANS

The first humans settled in what is now Tennessee 12,000-15,000 years ago. Descended from people who crossed into North America during the last ice age, these Paleo-Indians were nomads who hunted large game animals, including mammoth, mastodon, and caribou. Remains of these extinct mammals have been found in West Tennessee, and the Indians' arrowheads and spear points have been found all over the state. The ice age hunters camped in caves and under rock shelters but remained predominantly nomadic.

About 10,000 years ago, the climate and vegetation of the region changed. The deciduous forest that still covers large parts of the state replaced the evergreen forest of the fading ice age. Large game animals disappeared, and deer and elk arrived, attracted by the forests of hickory, chestnut, and beech. Descendants of the Paleo-Indians gradually abandoned the nomadic lifestyle of their ancestors and established settlements, often near rivers. They hunted deer, bear, and turkey; gathered nuts and wild fruit; and harvested freshwater fish and mussels. They also took a few tentative steps toward cultivation by growing squash and gourds.

This Archaic Period was replaced by the Woodland Period about 3,000 years ago. The Woodland Indians adopted the bow and arrow for hunting and—at the end of their predominance—began cultivating maize and beans as staple crops. Ceramic pottery appeared, and ritualism took on a greater importance in the society. Pinson Mounds, burial mounds near Jackson in West Tennessee, date from this period, as does the wrongly named Old Stone Fort near Manchester, believed to have been built and used for ceremonies by the Woodland Indians of the area.

The development of a more complex culture continued, and at about AD 900 the Woodland culture gave way to the Mississippian Period, an era marked by population growth, an increase in trade and warfare, the rise of the chieftain, and cultural accomplishments. The Mississippian era is best known for the impressive large pyramid mounds that were left behind in places such as Etowah and Toqua in Tennessee and Moundville in Alabama. Mississippian Indians also created beautiful ornaments and symbolic objects including combs, pipes, and jewelry.

Europeans Arrive

Having conquered Peru, the Spanish nobleman Hernando de Soto embarked on a search for gold in the American southeast in 1539. De Soto's band wandered through Florida, Georgia, and the Carolinas before crossing into what is now Tennessee, probably in June 1540. His exact route is a source of controversy, but historians believe he made his way through parts of East Tennessee before heading back into Georgia. The popular myth that he camped on the Chickasaw Bluff—the site of Memphis today—in 1541 remains unproven.

It was more than 100 years until another European was reported in the Tennessee wilderness, although life for the natives was already changing. De Soto and his men brought firearms and disease, and there was news of other whites living to the east. Disease and warfare led to a decline in population for Tennessee's Indians during the presettlement period. As a result, Indian communities formed new tribes with each other: The Creek Confederacy and Choctaws were among the tribes that were formed. In Tennessee, the Shawnee moved south into the Cumberland River country—land previously claimed as hunting ground by the Chickasaw Nation. Also at this time, a new tribe came over the Smoky Mountains from North Carolina, possibly to escape encroachment of European settlers, to form what would become the most important Indian group in modern Tennessee: the Overhill Cherokee.

In 1673, European scouts entered Tennessee at its eastern and western ends. Englishmen James Needham, Gabriel Arthur, and eight hired Indian guides were the first European party to enter East Tennessee. Needham did not last long; he was killed by his Indian guides early in the outing. Arthur won over his traveling companions and joined them on war trips and hunts before returning to Virginia in 1674. Meanwhile, on the western end of the state, French explorers Father Jacques Marquette and trader Louis Joliet came down the Mississippi River and claimed the surrounding valley for the French.

Nine years later, Robert Cavelier de La Salle paused at the Chickasaw Bluff near present-day Memphis and built Fort Prudhomme as a temporary base. The fort was short-lived, but the site would be used by the French in years to come in their war against the Chickasaws and later in the French and Indian War.

The Long Hunters

The first Europeans to carve out a foothold in the unknown frontier of Tennessee were traders who made journeys into Indian territory to hunt and trade. These men disappeared for months at a time into the wilderness and were therefore known as long hunters. They left with European-made goods and returned with animal skins. They led pack trains of horses and donkeys over narrow, steep, and crooked mountain trails and through sometimes-hostile territory. It was a lonely, hard life, full of uncertainty. Some of the long hunters were no better than crooks; others were respected by both the Indians and Europeans.

The long hunters included men like Elisha Walden, Kasper Mansker, and Abraham Bledsoe. Daniel Boone, born in North Carolina, was in present-day Washington County in northeastern Tennessee when, in 1760, he carved on a beech tree that he had "cilled" a "bar" nearby. Thomas Sharp

Spencer became known as Big Foot and is said to have spent the winter in a hollowed-out sycamore tree. Another trader, a Scotch-Irish man named James Adair, traded with the Indians for years and eventually wrote *A History of the American Indian,* published in London in 1775 and one of the first such accounts.

The animal skins and furs that were the aim of these men's exploits were eventually sold in Charleston and exported to Europe. In 1748 alone, South Carolina merchants exported more than 160,000 skins worth $250,000. The trade was profitable for merchants and, to a lesser extent, the traders themselves. But it was rarely profitable for the Indians, and it helped to wipe out much of Tennessee's native animal life.

The French and Indian War

In 1754, the contest between the French and the British for control of the New World boiled over into war. Indian alliances were seen as critical to success, and so the British set out to win the support of the Cherokee. They did this by agreeing to build a fort in the land over the mountain from North Carolina—territory that came to be known as the Overhill country. The Cherokee wanted the fort to protect their women and children from French or hostile-Indian attack while the men were away. The fort was begun in 1756 near the fork of the Little Tennessee and Tellico Rivers, and it was named Fort Loudoun after the commander of British forces in America. Twelve cannons were transported over the rough mountain terrain by horse to defend the fort from enemy attack.

The construction of Fort Loudoun did not prove to be the glue to hold the Cherokee and British together. In fact, it was not long before relations deteriorated to the point where the Cherokee chief Standing Turkey directed an attack on the fort. A siege ensued. Reinforcements were called for and dispatched, but the British colonel and 1,300 men turned back before reaching the fort. The English inside the fort were weakened by lack of food and surrendered. On August 9, 1760, 180 men, 60 women, and a few children marched out of Fort Loudoun, the first steps of a 140-mile journey to the nearest British fort. The group had been promised to be allowed to retreat peacefully, but on the first night of the journey the group was ambushed: killed were 3 officers, 23 privates, 3 women. The rest were taken prisoner. The Indians said they were inspired to violence upon finding that the British had failed to surrender all of their firepower as promised.

The Cherokee's action was soon avenged. A year later, Col. James Grant led a party into the Lower Cherokee territory, where they destroyed villages, burnt homes, and cut down fields of corn.

The French and Indian War ended in 1763, and in the Treaty of Paris the French withdrew any claims to lands east of the Mississippi. This result emboldened European settlers and land speculators who were drawn to the land of the Overhill country. The fact that the land still belonged to the Indians did not stop the movement west.

EARLY SETTLERS
The First Settlements

With the issue of French possession resolved, settlers began to filter into the Overhill country. Early settlers included William Bean, on the Holston River; Evan Shelby, at Sapling Grove (later Bristol); John Carter, in the Carter Valley; and Jacob Brown, on the Nolichucky River. By 1771, the settlers at Wataugua and Nolichucky won a lease from the Cherokee, and the next year, they formed the Watauga Association, a quasi government and the first such in Tennessee territory.

The settlers' success in obtaining land concessions from the Indians was eclipsed in 1775 when the Transylvania Company, led by Richard Henderson of North Carolina, traded £10,000 of goods for 20 million acres of land in Kentucky and Tennessee. The agreement, negotiated at a treaty conference at Sycamore Shoals, was opposed by the Cherokee chief Dragging Canoe, who warned that the Cherokee were paving the way for their own extinction. Despite his warning, the treaty was signed.

Dragging Canoe remained the leader of the Cherokee's resistance to European settlement. In 1776, he orchestrated assaults on the white settlements of Watauga, Nolichucky, Long Island, and Carter's Valley. The offensive, called by some the Cherokee War, had limited success at first, but it ended in defeat for the natives. In 1777, the Cherokee signed a peace treaty with the settlers that ceded more land to the Europeans.

Dragging Canoe and others did not accept the treaty and left the Cherokee as a result. He and his followers moved south, near Chickamauga Creek, where they became known as the Chickamauga tribe. Over time, this tribe attracted other Indians whose common purpose was opposition to white settlement.

The Indians could not, however, overpower the increasing tide of European settlers, who brought superior firepower and greater numbers. Pressure on political leaders to free up more and more land for settlement made relations with the Indians and land agreements with them one of the most important features of political life on the frontier.

In the end, these leaders delivered. Europeans obtained Indian land in Tennessee through a series of treaties and purchases, beginning with the Sycamore Shoals purchase in 1775 and continuing until 1818, when the Chickasaw ceded all control to land west of the Mississippi. Negotiating on behalf of the settlers were leaders including William Blount, the territorial governor, and Andrew Jackson, the first U.S. president from Tennessee.

Indian Removal

Contact with Europeans had a significant impact on the Cherokee's way of life. Christian missionaries introduced education, and in the 1820s, Sequoyah developed a Cherokee alphabet, allowing the Indians to read and write in their own language. The Cherokee adopted some of the Europeans' farming practices, as well as some of their social practices, including slavery. Adoption of the European lifestyle was most common among the significant number of mixed-race Cherokee. In 1827, the Cherokee Nation was established, complete with a constitutional system of government and a capital in New Echota, Georgia. From 1828 until 1832, its newspaper, the *Cherokee Phoenix,* was published in both English and Cherokee.

The census of 1828 counted 15,000 Cherokee remaining in Tennessee. They owned 1,000 slaves, 22,400 head of cattle, 7,600 horses, 1,800 spinning wheels, 700 looms, 12 sawmills, 55 blacksmith shops, and 6 cotton gins.

Despite these beginnings of assimilation, or because of them, the Cherokee were not welcome to remain in the new territory. Settlers pushed for a strong policy that would lead to the Cherokee's removal, and they looked over the border to Georgia to see that it could be done. There, in 1832, authorities surveyed lands owned by Cherokee and disposed of them by lottery. Laws were passed to prohibit Indian assemblies and bar Indians from bringing suit in the state. The majority of Tennessee settlers, as well as Georgia officials, pushed for similar measures to be adopted in Tennessee.

The Cherokee were divided in their response: Some felt that moving west represented the best future for their tribe, while others wanted to stay and fight for their land and the Cherokee Nation. In the end, the Cherokee leaders lost hope of remaining, and on December 29, 1835, they signed the removal treaty. Under the agreement, the Cherokee were paid $5 million for all their lands east of the Mississippi, and they were required to move west within two years. When that time expired in 1838 and only a small number of the Cherokee had moved, the U.S. army evicted the rest by force.

Thousands of Cherokee died along the ensuing Trail of Tears, which followed four different routes through Tennessee and eventually into Oklahoma: A southern route extended from Chattanooga to Memphis, two northern routes headed into Kentucky and Missouri before turning southward into Oklahoma, and the fourth was a water route along the Tennessee and Mississippi Rivers. Harsh weather, food shortages, and the brutality of the journey cost thousands of Cherokee lives. In the end, out of the estimated 14,000 Cherokee who began the journey, more than 4,000 are believed to have died along the way.

Some Cherokee remained by hiding deep in the Great Smoky Mountains. Later, they were given land that became the Cherokee Reservation in North Carolina.

STATEHOOD

Almost as soon as settlers began living on the Tennessee frontier there were movements to form a government. Dissatisfied with the protection offered by North Carolina's distant government, settlers drew up their own governments as early as the 1780s. The Watauga Association and Cumberland Compact were early forms of government. In 1785, settlers in northeastern Tennessee seceded from North Carolina and established the State of Franklin. The experiment was short-lived but foretold that in the future the lands west of the Smoky Mountains would be their own state.

Before Tennessee could become a state, however, it was a territory of the

United States. In 1789, North Carolina ratified its own constitution and in doing so ceded its western lands, the Tennessee country, to the U.S. government. These lands eventually became known as the Southwest Territory, and in 1790, President George Washington appointed William Blount its territorial governor.

Blount was a 41-year-old land speculator and businessman who had campaigned actively for the position. A veteran of the War for Independence, Blount knew George Washington and was one of the signers of the U.S. Constitution in 1787.

At the time of its establishment, the Southwest Territory was 43,000 square miles in area. The population of 35,000 was centered in two main areas: the northeastern corner and the Cumberland settlements near present-day Nashville.

Governor Blount moved quickly to establish a territorial government. In October 1790, he arrived in Washington County and established the state's first capitol in the home of William Cobb. This simple wood-frame house, known as Rocky Mount, would be the territory's capitol for the next 18 months before it moved to James White's Fort in Knoxville.

The territory's first election was held in 1793, and the resulting council met a year later. They established the town of Knoxville, created a tax rate, and chartered Greeneville and Blount Colleges. They also ordered a census in 1795, which showed a population of more than 77,000 people and support for statehood.

The territory had met the federal requirements for statehood, and so Blount and other territorial leaders set out to make Tennessee a state. They called a constitutional convention, and delegates spent three weeks writing Tennessee's first constitution. The first statewide poll elected John Sevier governor of the new state. Meanwhile, Tennessee's request to become a state was being debated in Washington, where finally, on June 1, 1796, President Washington signed the statehood bill and Tennessee became the 16th state in the Union.

Frontier Life

The new state of Tennessee attracted settlers who were drawn by cheap land and the opportunity it represented. Between 1790 and 1800, the state's population tripled, and by 1810, Tennessee's population had grown to 250,000. The expansion caused a shift in power as the middle and western parts of the state became more populated. The capital moved from Knoxville to Nashville in 1812.

Life during the early 19th century in Tennessee was largely rural. For the subsistence farmers who made up the majority of the state's population, life was a relentless cycle of hard work. Many families lived in one- or two-room cabins and spent their days growing food and the fibers needed to make their own clothes; raising animals that supplied farm power, meat, and hides; building or repairing buildings and tools; and cutting firewood in prodigious quantities.

Small-hold farmers often owned no slaves. Those who did only owned one or two and worked alongside them.

Children provided valuable labor on the Tennessee farm. Boys often plowed their first furrow at age nine, and girls of that age were expected to mind younger children, help cook, and learn the skills of midwifery, sewing, and gardening. While women's time was often consumed with child rearing, cooking, and sewing, the housewife worked in the field alongside her husband when she was needed.

Education and Religion

There were no public schools on the frontier, and the few private schools that existed were not accessible to the farming class. Religious missionaries were often the only people who could read and write in a community, and the first schools were established by churches. Presbyterian, Methodist, and Baptist ministers were the first to reach many settlements in Tennessee.

Settlements were spread out, and few had established churches. As a result, the camp meeting became entrenched in Tennessee culture. The homegrown spirituality of the camp meeting appealed to Tennesseans' independent spirit, which looked suspiciously at official religion and embraced the informal and deeply personal religion of the camp meeting.

The meetings were major events drawing between a few hundred and thousands of people. Wilma Dykeman writes:

From distances as far as 40, 50 and more miles, they came in wagons, carriages, a wide array of vehicles, and raised their tents. . . . They spent the summer days and nights surrounded by seemingly endless expanse of green forest, supplied with a bounty of cold pure water, breathing that acrid blue wood smoke from rows of campfires and the rich smells of food cooking over glowing red coals, listening to the greetings of old friends, the voices of children playing, crying, growing drowsy, a stamping of the horses, and the bedlam of the meeting itself once the services had begun.

Camp services were passionate and emotional, reaching a feverish pitch as men and women were overtaken by the spirit. Many camp meetings attracted both black and white participants.

The War of 1812

Tennesseans were among the "War Hawks" in Congress who advocated for war with Great Britain in 1812. The conflict was seen by many as an opportunity to rid their borders once and for all of Indians. The government asked for 2,800 volunteers, and 30,000 Tennesseans offered to enlist. This is when Tennessee's nickname as the Volunteer State was born.

Nashville lawyer, politician, and businessman Andrew Jackson was chosen as the leader of the Tennessee volunteers. Despite their shortage of supplies and lack of support from the War Department, Jackson's militia prevailed in a series of lopsided victories. Given command of the southern military district, Andrew Jackson led U.S. forces at the Battle of New Orleans on January 8, 1815. The ragtag group inflicted a crushing defeat on the British, and despite having occurred after the signing of the peace treaty with Great Britain, the battle was a victory that launched Jackson onto the road to the presidency.

Growth of Slavery

The state's first settlers planted the seed of slavery in Tennessee, and the state's westward expansion cemented the institution. In 1791, there were 3,400 blacks in Tennessee—about 10 percent of the general population. By 1810, blacks were more than 20 percent of Tennessee's people. The invention of the cotton gin and subsequent rise of King Cotton after the turn of the 19th century also caused a rapid expansion of slavery.

Slavery was most important in West Tennessee; eastern Tennessee, with its mountainous landscape and small farms, had the fewest slaves. In Middle Tennessee the slave population was concentrated in the central basin, in the counties of Davidson, Maury, Rutherford, and Williamson. By 1860, 40 percent of the state's slave population was in West Tennessee, with the greatest concentration in Shelby, Fayette, and Haywood Counties, where cotton was grown on plantations somewhat similar to those of the Deep South.

As slavery grew, slave markets were established in Nashville and Memphis. The ban on the interstate sale of slaves was virtually ignored.

From 1790, when the state was founded, until 1831, Tennessee's slave code was relatively lenient. The law recognized a slave as both a chattel and a person, and slaves were entitled to expect protection against the elements and other people. Owners could free their slaves for any reason, and many did, causing growth in Tennessee's free black population in the first half of the 1800s. These free blacks concentrated in eastern and Middle Tennessee, and particularly the cities of Nashville, Memphis, and Knoxville, where they worked as laborers and artisans.

There were vocal opponents to slavery in Tennessee, particularly in the eastern part of the state. The first newspaper in the United States devoted to emancipation was established in 1819 in Jonesborough by Elihu Embree. Charles Osborne, a Quaker minister, preached against slavery shortly after the turn of the 19th century in Tennessee. Emancipationists formed societies in counties that included Washington, Sullivan, Blount, Grainger, and Cocke. Many of these early abolitionists opposed slavery on religious grounds, arguing that it was incompatible with the spirit of Christianity.

These abolitionists often argued for the gradual end of slavery and sometimes advocated for the removal of freed slaves to Africa.

Slave Experiences

There was no single slave experience for Tennessee's slaves. On the farm, a slave's experience depended on the size of the farm, the type of crops that were grown, and the number of slaves on the farm.

Most Tennessee slaves lived on small- or medium-size farms. The 1860 census showed that only one person in the state owned more than 300 slaves, and 47 owned more than 100. More than 75 percent of all slave owners had fewer than 10 slaves. Work assignments varied, but almost all slaves were expected to contribute to their own subsistence by keeping a vegetable garden. Slaves with special skills in areas like carpentry, masonry, blacksmithing, or weaving were hired out.

Urban slaves were domestics, coachmen, house painters, laundresses, and midwives. In cities, many families owned just one or two slaves, and it was common for slaves to be hired out to others in order to provide a source of income for the slave owner. It became customary in some cities for a market day to be held on New Year's Day, when employers bargained for slave labor over the coming year.

Slaves sought to overcome their circumstances by building close-knit communities. These communities acted as surrogate families for slaves whose own spouse, parents, siblings, and children were often sold, causing lifelong separation.

Religion also served as a survival mechanism for Tennessee's slaves. Methodist and Baptist churches opened their doors to slaves, providing a space were slaves could be together. The musical tradition that resulted is today's gospel music. Religion also provided a vehicle for some slaves to learn how to read and write.

BACKGROUND HISTORY

THE CIVIL WAR

In the 1830s, Tennessee's position on slavery hardened. The Virginia slave uprising led by Nat Turner frightened slave owners, who instituted patrols to search for runaway slaves and tightened codes on slave conduct. In 1834, the state constitution was amended to bar free blacks from voting, a sign of whites' increasing fear of the black people living in their midst.

The division between East and West Tennessee widened as many in the east were sympathetic with the antislavery forces that were growing in Northern states. In the west, the support for slavery was unrelenting.

Despite several strident secessionists, including Tennessee governor Isham Harris, Tennessee remained uncertain about secession. In February 1861, the state voted against a convention on secession. But with the attack on Fort Sumter two months later, followed by President Abraham Lincoln's call for volunteers to coerce the seceded states back to the Union, public opinion shifted. On June 8, 1861, Tennesseans voted 105,000 to 47,000 to secede.

A Border State

Tennessee was of great strategic importance during the Civil War. It sent an estimated 186,000 men to fight for the Confederacy, more than any other state. Another 31,000 are credited with having joined the Union army.

Tennessee had resources that both Union and Confederacy deemed important for victory, including agricultural and manufacturing industries, railroads, and rivers. And its geographic position as a long-border state made it nearly unavoidable.

Some 454 battles and skirmishes were fought in Tennessee during the war. Most were small, but several key battles took place on Tennessee soil.

The first of these was the Union victory at Forts Henry and Donelson in January 1862. Gen. Ulysses S. Grant and 15,000 Union troops steamed up the Tennessee River and quickly captured Fort Henry. They then marched overland to Fort Donelson, and, 10 days later, this Confederate fort fell as well. The battle of Fort Donelson is where U. S. Grant earned his sobriquet: He was asked by the Confederate general the terms of capitulation, and he replied, "unconditional surrender."

The Battle of Shiloh was the bloodiest and largest confrontation in Tennessee. The battle took place near Pittsburgh Landing (the Federal name for the struggle), on the Mississippi River about 20 miles north of the Mississippi state line. More than 100,000 men took part in this battle, and there were more than 24,000 casualties.

The battle began with a surprise Confederate attack at dawn on April 6, 1862, a Sunday. For several hours, victory seemed in reach for the Southern troops, but the Union rallied and held. They built a strong defensive line covering Pittsburgh Landing, and on April 7 they took the offensive and swept the Confederates from the field. The Confederates' loss was devastating, and Shiloh represents a harbinger of the future bloodletting between Blue and Gray.

Another important Tennessee battle was at Stones River, near Murfreesboro, on December 31, 1862. Like at Shiloh, the early momentum here was with the Confederates, but victory belonged to the Union. The Battle of Chickamauga Creek, fought a few miles over the state line in Georgia, was a rare Confederate victory. It did not come cheaply, however, with 21,000 members of the Army of Tennessee killed.

Federal forces retreated and dug in near Chattanooga, while Confederates occupied the heights above the town. Union reinforcements

view of the state capitol near the end of the Civil War

BACKGROUND
HISTORY

led by General Grant drove the Confederates back into Georgia at Battle of Lookout Mountain, also known as the "Battle Above the Clouds," on November 25, 1863.

Wartime Occupation

Battles were only part of the wartime experience in Tennessee. The Civil War caused hardship for ordinary residents on a scale that many had never before seen. There was famine and poverty. Schools and churches were closed. Harassment and recrimination plagued the state, and fear was widespread.

In February 1863, one observer described the population of Memphis as "11,000 original whites, 5,000 slaves, and 19,000 newcomers of all kinds, including traders, fugitives, hangers-on, and negroes."

Memphis fell to the Union on June 6, 1862, and it was occupied for the remainder of the war. The city's experience during this wartime occupation reversed decades of growth and left a city that would struggle for years.

Those who could, fled the city. Many of those who remained stopped doing business (some of these because they refused to pledge allegiance to the Union and were not permitted). Northern traders entered the city and took over many industries, while blacks who abandoned nearby plantations flooded into the city.

While the military focused on punishing Confederate sympathizers, conditions in Memphis deteriorated. Crime and disorder abounded, and guerrilla bands developed to fight the Union occupation. The Federal commander responsible for the city was Maj. Gen. William T. Sherman, and he adopted a policy of collective responsibility, which held civilians responsible for guerrilla attacks in their neighborhoods. Sherman destroyed hundreds of homes, farms, and towns in the exercise of this policy.

The war was equally damaging in other parts of Tennessee. In Middle Tennessee, retreating Confederate soldiers after the fall of Fort Donelson demolished railroads and burned bridges so as not to leave them for the Union. Union troops also destroyed and appropriated the region's resources. Federals took horses, pigs, cows, corn, hay, cotton, fence rails, firearms, and tools. Sometimes this was carried out through official requisitions, but at other times it amounted to little more than pillaging.

Criminals took advantage of the loss of public order, and bands of thieves and bandits began roaming the countryside.

The experience in East Tennessee was different. Because of the region's widespread Union sympathies, it was the Confederacy that first occupied the eastern territory. During this time, hundreds of alleged Unionists were charged with treason and jailed. When the Confederates began conscripting men into military service in 1862, tensions in East Tennessee grew. Many East Tennesseans fled to Kentucky, and distrust, bitterness, and violence escalated. In September 1863, the tables turned, however, and the Confederates were replaced by the Federals, whose victories elsewhere enabled them to now focus on occupying friendly East Tennessee.

The Effects of the War

Tennessee lost most of a generation of young men to the Civil War. Infrastructure was destroyed, and thousands of farms, homes, and other properties were razed. The state's reputation on the national stage had been tarnished, and it would be decades until Tennessee had the political power that it enjoyed during the Age of Jackson. But while the war caused tremendous hardships for the state, it also led to the freeing of 275,000 black Tennesseans from slavery.

RECONSTRUCTION

Tennessee was no less divided during the years following the Civil War than it was during the conflict. The end to the war ushered in a period where former Unionists—now allied with the Radical Republicans in Congress—disenfranchised and otherwise marginalized former Confederates and others who had been sympathetic with the Southern cause.

They also pushed through laws that extended voting and other rights to the newly freed blacks, changes that led to a powerful backlash and the establishment of such shadowy groups as the Ku Klux Klan (KKK).

William G. "Parson" Brownlow of Knoxville, a vocal supporter of the Union, was elected governor of Tennessee in 1865. During the same year, the voters approved a constitutional amendment abolishing slavery, making Tennessee the only seceded state to abolish slavery by its own act. Brownlow and his supporters bent laws and manipulated loyalties in order to secure ratification of the 14th and 15th Amendments to the constitution, paving the way for Tennessee to be admitted back to the Union, the first Southern state to be readmitted following the war. Brownlow's success ensured that Tennessee would not experience the congressionally mandated Reconstruction that other former Confederate states did.

Recognizing that the unpopularity of his positions among Tennessee's numerous former Confederates placed his political future in jeopardy,

General Ulysses S. Grant (lower left-hand corner) visits Missionary Ridge, scene of a Civil War battle.

Brownlow and his supporters extended the right to vote to thousands of freedmen in February 1867. During the statewide vote a few months later, Brownlow and his followers were swept to victory, largely due to the support of black voters.

The quick rise to power of former enemies and the social changes caused by the end of slavery led some former Confederates to bitterness and frustration. In the summer of 1867, the Ku Klux Klan emerged as a political and terrorist movement to keep freedmen in their traditional place. Klan members initially concerned themselves principally with supporting former Confederates and their families, but they were soon known more for their attacks on black men and women. The KKK was strongest in Middle and West Tennessee, except for a small pocket near Bristol in East Tennessee.

Governor Brownlow responded strongly to the KKK's activities, and in 1869, he declared martial law in nine counties where the organization was most active. But when Brownlow left Tennessee shortly thereafter to fill a seat in the U.S. Senate, the KKK's grand wizard, former Confederate general Nathan Bedford Forrest, declared the group's mission accomplished and encouraged members to burn their robes. The KKK's influence quickly faded, only to reemerge 50 years later at Stone Mountain, Georgia.

Brownlow was replaced by Senate Speaker Dewitt C. Senter, who quickly struck a more moderate position than his predecessor by setting aside the law that had barred Confederate veterans from voting.

The greatest legacy of the Civil War was the emancipation of Tennessee's slaves. Following the war, many freed blacks left the countryside and moved to cities, including Memphis, Nashville, Chattanooga, and Knoxville, where they worked as skilled laborers, domestics, and more. Other blacks remained in the countryside, working as wage laborers on farms or sharecropping in exchange for occupancy on part of a former large-scale plantation.

The Freedmen's Bureau worked in Tennessee for a short period after the end of the war, and it succeeded in establishing schools for blacks. During this period the state's first black colleges were inaugurated: Fisk, Tennessee Central, LeMoyne, Roger Williams, Lane, and Knoxville.

As in other states, blacks in Tennessee enjoyed short-lived political power during Reconstruction. The right to vote and the concentration of blacks in certain urban areas paved the way for blacks to be elected to the Tennessee House of Representatives, beginning with Sampson Keeble of Nashville in 1872. In all, 13 blacks were elected as representatives between 1872 and 1887, including James C. Napier, Edward Shaw, and William Yardley, who also ran for governor.

Initially, these pioneers met mild acceptance from whites, but as time progressed whites became uncomfortable sharing political power with black people. By the 1890s, racist Jim Crow policies of segregation, poll taxes, secret ballots, literacy tests, and intimidation prevented blacks from holding elective office—and in many cases, voting—in Tennessee again until after the civil rights movement of the 1960s.

The Republican Party saw the end of its influence with the end of the Brownlow governorship. Democrats rejected the divisive policies of the Radical Republicans, sought to protect the racial order that set blacks at a disadvantage to whites, and were less concerned about the state's mounting debt than the Republicans.

Economic Recovery

The social and political upheaval caused by the Civil War was matched or exceeded by the economic catastrophe that it represented for the state. Farms and industry were damaged or destroyed, public infrastructure was razed, schools were closed, and the system of slavery that underpinned most of the state's economy was gone.

The economic setback was seen as an opportunity by proponents of the "New South," who advocated for an industrial and economic revival that would catapult the South to prosperity impossible under the agrarian and slavery-based antebellum economy. The New South movement was personified by carpetbagging Northern capitalists who moved to Tennessee and set up industries that would benefit from cheap labor and abundant natural resources. Many Tennesseans welcomed these newcomers and advocated for their fellow Tennesseans to put aside regional differences and welcome the Northern investors.

The result was an array of industries that were chartered during the years following the Civil War. Mining, foundries, machine shops, sawmills, gristmills, furniture factories, and textile and other manufacturing industries were established. Knoxville and Chattanooga improved quickly. Over the 10-year period from 1860 to 1870, Chattanooga's industrial works grew from employing 214 men to more than 2,000.

Memphis and Nashville also worked to attract industries. Memphis was on the cusp of a commercial and industrial boom in 1873 when yellow fever hit the city; the epidemic caused widespread death and hurt Memphis's economic recovery. In Nashville, new distilleries, sawmills, paper mills, stove factories, and an oil refinery led the way to industrialization.

Industry also settled in the small towns and countryside. The coal-rich region of the Cumberland Mountains was the site of major coal-mining operations. Copper mines were opened in Cleveland, flouring mills in Jackson, and textile factories in Tullahoma and other parts of the state.

Agriculture

A revolution was brewing in agriculture, too. Civil War veterans returned to small farms all over the state and resumed farming with implements largely unchanged for hundreds of years. Every task was achieved by hand, with the lone help of one or two farm animals.

But farm technology was beginning to change. Thirty years after the war, new labor-saving devices began to be put to use. These included early cotton pickers, reapers, and planters. Seed cleaners, corn shellers, and improved plows were made available. In 1871 the state formed the Bureau of

Agriculture, whose employees prepared soil maps and studied the state's climate, population, and the prices of land. New methods such as crop diversification, crop rotation, cover crops, and the use of commercial fertilizers were introduced, and farmers were encouraged to use them.

Meanwhile, farmers themselves established a strong grassroots movement in the state. The Patrons of Husbandry, or the Grange, was organized shortly after the war to encourage members to improve farming methods and enhance their economic influence. Government encouraged county fair associations, which organized fairs where farmers could be awarded for their crops and encouraged to use new farming methods. The Farmers' Alliance and the Agricultural Wheel, both national organizations, grew in prominence in the 1880s and advocated currency reform, empowerment of farmers, and control of communication and transportation systems. The Alliance gave low-interest loans to farmers and encouraged cooperative selling.

While the Alliance and the Wheel were not political organizations as such, they supported candidates who adopted their views on agricultural matters. In 1890, the Alliance supported Democrat John P. Buchanan for governor, and he was successful. For their part, political elites did not take the farming movement or its leaders very seriously, ridiculing them as "hayseeds," "clodhoppers," and "wool-hat boys." In other places, rural and small-town residents resisted the Wheel and the Alliance, in part because they feared challenge of the status quo. As the Alliance became more radical in its views, the support in Tennessee dwindled, and by 1892 it had faded in many parts of the state.

While some blacks remained on farms as wage laborers or sharecroppers, many left for the cities, causing a labor shortage. Attempts to attract foreign or Northern immigrants to the state were unsuccessful. Tennessee's poor whites filled this labor shortage, now able to own or rent land for the first time.

Education

Despite popular attempts and pleas by some politicians for a sound education system, Tennessee lagged behind in public education during the postwar years. In 1873, the legislature passed a school law that set up a basic framework of school administration, but the state's debt and financial problems crippled the new system. Private funds stepped in—the Peabody Fund contributed to Tennessee's schools, including the old University of Nashville, renamed Peabody after its benefactor. Meanwhile, teachers' institutes were established during the 1880s in order to raise the level of instruction at Tennessee's public schools.

PROHIBITION

Prohibition was the first major issue Tennesseans faced in the new century. An 1877 law that forbade the sale of alcohol within four miles of a rural school had been used to great effect by Prohibitionists to restrict the sale and traffic of alcohol in towns all over the countryside. As the century turned, pressure mounted to extend the law, and public opinion in support of temperance grew, although it was never without contest from the powerful distillery industry. Finally, in 1909, the legislature passed the Manufacturer's Bill, which would halt the production of intoxicants in the state and overrode Governor Patterson's veto. When the United States followed suit with the 18th Amendment in 1920, Prohibition was old news in Tennessee.

WORLD WAR I

True to its nickname, Tennessee sent a large number of volunteer troops to fight in World War I. Most became part of the 30th "Old Hickory" Division, which entered the war on August 17, 1918. The most famous Tennessee veteran of World War I was Alvin C. York, a farm boy from the Cumberland Mountains who staged a one-man offensive against the German army after becoming separated from his own detachment. Reports say that York killed 20 German soldiers and persuaded 131 more to surrender.

WOMEN'S SUFFRAGE

The movement for women's suffrage had been established in Tennessee prior to the turn of the 20th century, and it gained influence as the century progressed. The Southern Woman Suffrage Conference was held in Memphis in 1906, and a statewide suffrage organization was established. State bills to give women the right to vote failed in 1913 and 1917, but support was gradually growing. In the summer of 1920, the 19th Amendment had been ratified by 35 states, and one more ratification was needed to make it law. Tennessee was one of five states yet to vote on the measure, and on August 9, Democratic Governor Albert H. Roberts called a special sitting of the legislature to consider the amendment.

Furious campaigning and public debate led up to the special sitting. The Senate easily ratified the amendment 25 to 4, but in the House of Representatives the vote was much closer: 49 to 47. Governor Roberts certified the result and notified the secretary of state: Tennessee had cast the deciding vote for women's suffrage.

AUSTIN PEAY

The 1920s were years of growth and development in Tennessee, thanks in part to the capable leadership of Austin Peay, elected governor in 1922. He reformed the state government, cut waste, and set out to improve the state's roads and schools. The improvements won Peay support from the state's rural residents, who benefited from better transportation and education. Spending on schools doubled during Peay's three terms as governor, and the school term increased from 127 to 155 days per year.

Peay also saw the importance of establishing parks: Reelfoot Lake State Park was established during his third term, finally ending fears of development in the area. Peay also supported establishment of the Great Smoky

Mountains National Park, and he raised $1.5 million in a bond issue as the state's part toward the purchase of the land. Peay was dead by the time the park was opened in 1940, but it is largely to his credit that it was created.

THE DEPRESSION

The progress and hope of the 1920s was soon forgotten with the Great Depression. Tennessee's economic hard times started before the 1929 stock market crash. Farming in the state was hobbled by low prices and low returns during the 1920s. Farmers and laborers displaced by this trend sought work in new industries like the DuPont plant in Old Hickory, Eastman-Kodak in Kingsport, or the Aluminum Company of America in Blount County. But others, including many African Americans, left Tennessee for northern cities such as Chicago.

The Depression made bad things worse. Farmers tried to survive, turning to subsistence farming. In cities unemployed workers lined up for relief. Major bank failures in 1930 brought most financial business in the state to a halt.

President Franklin D. Roosevelt's New Deal provided some relief for Tennesseans. The Civilian Conservation Corps (CCC), Public Works Administration (PWA), and Civil Works Administration (CWA) were established in Tennessee. Through the CCC, more than 7,000 Tennesseans planted millions of pine seedlings, developed parks, and built fire towers. Through the PWA, more than 500 projects were undertaken, including bridges, housing, water systems, and roads. Hundreds of Tennesseans were employed by the CWA to clean public buildings, landscape roads, and do other work.

But no New Deal institution had more impact on Tennessee than the Tennessee Valley Authority. Architects of the TVA saw it as a way to improve agriculture along the Tennessee River, alleviate poverty, and produce electrical power. The dam system would also improve navigation along what was then an often dangerous river. The law establishing TVA was introduced by Senator George W. Norris of Nebraska and passed in 1933. Soon after, dams were under construction, and trade on the river increased due to improved navigability. Even more importantly, electric power was now so cheap that even Tennesseans in remote parts of the state could afford it. By 1945, TVA was the largest electrical utility in the nation, and new industries were attracted by cheap energy and improved transportation. Tourists also came to enjoy the so-called Great Lakes of the South.

The TVA story is not without its losers, however. TVA purchased or condemned more than one million acres of land and flooded 300,000 acres more, forcing 14,000 families to be displaced.

THE CRUMP MACHINE

The 1930s in Tennessee was the age of Ed Crump, Memphis's longtime mayor and political boss. The son of a former Confederate, Crump was born in Mississippi in 1874 and moved to Memphis when he was 17 years old. First elected in 1909 as a city councilman, Crump was a genius of human nature and organization. Able to assure statewide candidates the support of influential Shelby County, Crump's power extended beyond Memphis. His political power often required corruption, patronage, and the loss of individual freedoms. To get ahead, you had to pay homage to Boss Crump. He was particularly popular during the Depression, when constituents and others looked to Crump for much-needed relief.

Crump manipulated the votes in his home Shelby County by paying the $2 poll tax for cooperative voters. He allied with black leaders such as Robert Church Jr. to win support in the black community of Memphis.

WORLD WAR II

Tennessee, like the rest of the country, was changed by World War II. The war effort transformed the state's economy and led to a migration to the cities unprecedented in Tennessee's history. The tiny mountain town of Oak Ridge became the state's fifth-largest city almost overnight, and it is synonymous with the atomic bomb that was dropped on Hiroshima, Japan, at the final stage of the war.

More than 300,000 Tennesseans served in World War II and just under 6,000 died. During the war, Camps Forrest, Campbell, and Tyson served as prisoner-of-war camps. Several hundred war refugees settled in Tennessee, many in the Nashville area.

The war also sped up Tennessee's industrialization. Industrial centers in Memphis, Chattanooga, and Knoxville converted to war production, while new industries were established in smaller cities such as Kingsport. Agriculture was no longer Tennessee's most important economic activity. The industrial growth was a catalyst for urbanization. Nashville's population grew by 25 percent during the war, and Shelby County's by 35 percent. During the war, the Great Depression finally came to an end and women were brought into the workplace.

Tennesseans supported the war not only by volunteering to serve overseas, but on the home front as well. Families planted victory gardens, invested in war bonds, and supported soldiers.

Tennesseans served with distinction during the war. Cordell Hull, a native of Pickett County, was U.S. secretary of state for 12 years and is known as the Father of the United Nations for his role in drawing up the foundation of that institution.

POSTWAR TENNESSEE

Tennessee's industrialization continued after the war. By 1960, there were more city dwellers than rural dwellers in the state, and Tennessee was ranked the 16th most industrialized state in the United States. Industry that had developed during the war transformed to peacetime operation.

Ex-servicemen were not content with the political machines that had controlled Tennessee politics for decades. In 1948 congressman Estes Kefauver won a U.S. Senate seat, defeating the candidate chosen by

Memphis mayor Ed Crump. The defeat signaled an end to Crump's substantial influence in statewide elections. In 1953, Tennessee repealed the state poll tax, again limiting politicians' ability to manipulate the vote. The tide of change also swept in Senator Albert Gore Sr. and Governor Frank Clement in 1952. Kefauver, Gore, and Clement were moderate Democrats of the New South.

CIVIL RIGHTS

The early gains for blacks during Reconstruction were lost during the decades that followed. Segregation, the threat of violence, poll taxes, and literacy tests discriminated against blacks in all spheres of life: economic, social, political, and educational. The fight to right these wrongs was waged by many brave Tennesseans.

Early civil rights victories in Tennessee included the 1905 successful boycott of Nashville's segregated streetcars and the creation of a competing black-owned streetcar company. In the 1920s in Chattanooga, blacks successfully defeated the Ku Klux Klan at the polls. Black institutions of learning persevered in educating young African Americans and developing a generation of leaders.

Following World War II, there was newfound energy in the fight for civil rights. Returning black servicemen who had fought for their country demanded greater equality, and the opportunities of the age raised the stakes of economic equality. In 1946, racially based violence targeted at a returned black serviceman in Columbia brought national attention to violence against black citizens and raised awareness of the need to protect blacks' civil rights.

The Highlander Folk School, founded in Grundy County and later moved to Cocke County, was an important training center for community activists and civil rights leaders in the 1950s. Founder Miles Horton believed in popular education and sought to bring black and white activists together to share experiences. Many leaders in the national civil rights movement, including Rev. Martin Luther King Jr. and Rosa Parks, attended the folk school.

In the 1950s, the first steps toward public school desegregation took place in Tennessee. Following a lawsuit filed by black parents, Clinton desegregated its schools in 1956 on order of a federal court judge. The integration began peacefully, but outside agitators arrived to organize resistance, and in the end Governor Frank Clement was forced to call in 600 National Guardsmen to diffuse the violent atmosphere. But the first black students were allowed to stay, and in May 1957, Bobby Cain became the first African American to graduate from an integrated public high school in the South.

In the fall of 1957, Nashville's public schools were desegregated. As many as half of the white students stayed home in protest, and one integrated school, Hattie Cotton School, was dynamited and partially destroyed. Other Tennessee cities desegregated at a slower pace, and by 1960, only

169 of Tennessee's almost 150,000 black children of school age attended integrated schools.

The Nashville lunch counter sit-ins of 1960 were an important milestone in both the local and national civil rights movements. Led by students from the city's black universities, the sit-ins eventually forced an end to racial segregation of the city's public services. Over two months hundreds of black students were arrested for sitting at white-only downtown lunch counters. Black consumers' boycott of downtown stores put additional pressure on the business community. On April 19, thousands of protesters marched in silence to the courthouse to confront city officials, and the next day Rev. Martin Luther King Jr. addressed Fisk University. On May 10, 1960, several downtown stores integrated their lunch counters, and Nashville became the first major city in the South to begin desegregating its public facilities.

As the civil rights movement continued, Tennesseans played an important part. Tennesseans were involved with organizing the Student Nonviolent Coordinating Committee and participated in the Freedom Rides, which sought to integrate buses across the south. In 1965, A. W. Willis Jr. of Memphis became the first African American representative elected to the state's General Assembly in more than 60 years. Three years later, Memphis's sanitation workers went on strike to protest discriminatory pay and work rules. Dr. King came to Memphis to support the striking workers. On April 4, 1968, King was assassinated by a sniper as he stood on the balcony of the Lorraine Motel in downtown Memphis.

MODERN TENNESSEE

The industrialization that began during World War II has continued in modern-day Tennessee. In 1980, Nissan built what was then the largest truck assembly plant in the world at Smyrna, Tennessee. In 1987, Saturn Corporation chose Spring Hill as the site for its $2.1 billion automobile plant.

At the same time, however, the state's older industries—including textiles and manufacturing—have suffered losses over the past three decades, due in part to the movement of industry outside of the United States.

During the 1950s and beyond, Tennessee developed a reputation as a hotbed of musical talent. Memphis's Elvis Presley may have invented rock 'n' roll, and his Graceland mansion remains one of the state's most enduring tourist attractions. The Grand Ole Opry in Nashville was representative of a second musical genre that came to call Tennessee home: country music.

Government and Economy

GOVERNMENT

Tennessee is governed by its constitution, unchanged since 1870, when it was revised in light of emancipation, the Civil War, and Reconstruction.

Tennessee has a governor who is elected to four-year terms, a legislature, and court system. The lieutenant governor is not elected statewide; he or she is chosen by the Senate and also serves as its Speaker.

The legislature, or General Assembly, is made up of the 99-member House of Representatives and the 33-member Senate. The Tennessee State Supreme Court is made of five members, no two of whom can be from the same Grand Division. The Tennessee Supreme Court chooses the state's attorney general.

The executive branch consists of 21 cabinet-level departments, which employ 39,000 state workers. Departments are led by a commissioner who is appointed by the governor and serves as a member of his cabinet.

Tennessee has 95 counties; the largest is Shelby County, which contains Memphis. The smallest county by size is Trousdale, with 113 square miles; the smallest population is in Pickett County.

The state has 11 electoral college votes in U.S. presidential elections.

Modern Politics

Like other Southern states, Tennessee has seen a gradual shift to the political right since the 1960s. The shift began in 1966 with Howard Baker's election to the U.S. Senate, and it continued with Tennessee's support for Republican presidential candidate Richard Nixon in 1968 and 1972. Despite a few exceptions, the shift has continued into the 21st century, although Nashville, Memphis, and other parts of Middle and West Tennessee remain Democratic territory.

the state capitol and the downtown skyline in Nashville

East Tennessee holds the distinction as one of a handful of Southern territories that has consistently supported the Republican Party since the Civil War. Today, Republicans outpoll Democrats in this region by as much as three to one.

The statewide trend toward the Republican Party continued in 2008, with Tennessee being one of only a handful of states in which Democrat Barack Obama received a lesser proportion of votes than did Democrat Senator John Kerry four years earlier. State Republicans also succeeded in gaining control of both houses of the state legislature. The general shift to the right has continued in the governor's office. Previous governor Phil Bredesen is a Democrat, but he was succeeded by Republican Bill Haslam. Since 1967, no party has been able to keep the governor's seat for two terms.

Andrew Jackson may still be the most prominent Tennessean in American political history, but Tennessee politicians continue to play a role on the national stage. Albert Gore Jr., elected to the U.S. House of Representatives in 1976, served as vice president under Bill Clinton from 1992 until 2000, and he lost the hotly contested 2000 presidential contest to George W. Bush. Gore famously lost his home state to Bush, further evidence of Tennessee's move to the right. Gore went on to champion global climate change and win the Nobel Peace Prize, and he is often seen around Nashville.

Lamar Alexander, a former governor of Tennessee, was appointed secretary of education by President George H. W. Bush in 1990. Alexander—famous for his flannel shirts—ran unsuccessfully for president and was later elected senator from Tennessee. Bill Frist, a doctor, was also elected senator and rose to be the Republican majority leader during the presidency of George W. Bush, before quitting politics for medical philanthropy.

The most recent Tennessean to seek the Oval Office was former senator and *Law and Order* star Fred Thompson, now deceased, from Lewisburg in Middle Tennessee.

One of the most persistent political issues for Tennesseans in modern times has been the state's tax structure. The state first established a 2 percent sales tax in 1947, and it was increased incrementally over the years, eventually reaching 7 percent today. With local options, it is one of the highest sales tax rates in the country. (The state sales tax on food is 5.5 percent.) At the same time, the state has failed on more than one occasion—most recently during the second term of Republican governor Donald Sundquist in the late 1990s—to establish an income tax that would provide greater stability to the state's revenues.

Like much of the country, in 2008, Tennessee faced a serious budget crunch that led to the elimination of thousands of state jobs, cutbacks at state-funded universities, and the scaling back of the state health insurance program.

ECONOMY

Tennessee has the 18th-largest economy in the United States. Important industries include health care, education, farming, electrical power, and tourism. In the past few years, most job growth has been recorded in the areas of leisure, hospitality, education, and health care. Manufacturing, mining, and construction jobs have declined. Despite the overall slowing in manufacturing, there was good news in 2008 when Volkswagen announced that it chose Chattanooga as home for a new, $1 billion plant. That plant was expected to bring 2,000 jobs to the state and it started to make progress on those goals. In 2015 it came to light that 11 million Volkswagens were using software to overstate fuel efficiency. These actions may impact the automakers' future success in the state.

Tennessee's unemployment rate fluctuates but generally sits a half point above the national average.

About 17.6 percent of Tennessee families live in poverty, ranking the state 39th out of 50. The median household income is approximately $45,000.

All of Tennessee's cities have poverty rates higher than the state or national average. The percentage of Memphis families living below the poverty level is the state's highest: 26.9 percent of Memphis families are poor. The U.S. Census calls Memphis one of the poorest cities in the nation. Knoxville's family poverty rate is 21.3 percent.

Agriculture

Farming accounts for 14.2 percent, or $38.5 billion, of the Tennessee economy. More than 42 percent of the state's land is used in farming; 63.6 percent of this is cropland.

Soybeans, tobacco, corn, and hay are among Tennessee's most important agricultural crops. Cattle and calf production, chicken farming, and cotton cultivation are also important parts of the farm economy.

Greene County, in northeastern Tennessee, is the leading county for all types of cow farming; Giles and Lincoln Counties, in the south-central part of the state, rank second and third. The leading cotton producer is Haywood County, followed by Crockett and Gibson, all three of which are located in West Tennessee. Other counties where agriculture figures largely into the economy are Obion, Dyer, Rutherford, and Robertson.

Tennessee ranks sixth among U.S. states for equine production, and walking or quarter horses account for more than half of the state's estimated 210,000 head of equine. The state ranks third for tomatoes, fourth for tobacco, and seventh for cotton.

Some farmers have begun converting to corn production in anticipation of a biofuel boom.

Tourism

According to the state tourism department, the industry generated $16.7 billion in economic activity in 2013. More than 175,000 Tennessee jobs are linked to tourism. The state credits the industry with generating more than $1.3 billion in state and local tax revenue.

People and Culture

DEMOGRAPHICS

Tennessee is home to 6.6 million people. Almost one quarter of these are 18 years and younger; about 13 percent are older than 65. Tennessee is 79 percent white and 17 percent black.

Memphis counts 656,861 residents and is the state's largest city. More than 63 percent of Memphians are African American, a greater proportion than is found in any other American city. Memphis has the youngest average age of the major Tennessee cities.

RELIGION

Tennessee is unquestionably part of the U.S. Bible Belt; the conservative Christian faith is both prevalent and prominent all over the state. According to the 2015 Census, 82 percent of Tennesseans call themselves Christians, and 39 percent of these identify as Baptist. The second-largest Christian denomination is Methodist. Nashville is the headquarters of the Southern Baptist Convention, the National Baptist Convention, and the United Methodist Church. Memphis is the headquarters of the mostly African American Church of God in Christ. However, the state's major cities do have growing populations that practice Judaism and Islam.

While Tennessee's urban centers are the home of church headquarters, religious fervor is strongest in the rural communities. Pentecostal churches have been known for rites such as speaking in tongues and snake handling, although these activities are not as widespread as they once were.

Non-Christians will feel most comfortable in urban areas, where numbers of religious minorities have grown in recent years and where the influence of the local churches is not as great.

One practical effect of Tennessee's Christian bent is that many counties and even cities are totally dry, while most bar the sale of alcohol on Sunday.

LANGUAGE

Tennesseans speak English, of a kind. The Tennessee drawl varies from the language of the upper South, spoken in East Tennessee and closely associated with the region's Scotch-Irish roots, and the language of West Tennessee, more akin to that of Mississippi and the lower South.

Little in Tennesseans' speech is distinct to the state itself. Speech patterns heard in Tennessee are also heard in other states in the region.

Speech patterns that have been documented throughout the state, but that may be more prevalent in the east, include the following, outlined by Michael Montgomery of the University of South Carolina in the *Tennessee Encyclopedia of History and Culture*. Montgomery writes that Tennesseans tend to pronounce vowels in the words *pen* and *hem* as *pin* and *him*; they shift the accent to the beginning of words, so *Tennessee* becomes *TIN-i-see*; they clip or reduce the vowel in words like *ride* so it sounds more like *rad*; and vowels in other words are stretched, so that a single-syllable word like *bed* becomes *bay-ud*.

Tennessee speech patterns are not limited to word pronunciation. Tennesseans also speak with folksy and down-home language. Speakers often use colorful metaphors, and greater value is placed on the quality of expression than the perfection of grammar.

THE ARTS
Crafts

Many Tennessee craft traditions have their roots in the handmade housewares that rural families had to make for themselves, including things like quilts and coverlets, baskets, candles, and furniture. These items were fashioned out of materials that could be raised or harvested nearby, and colors were derived from natural dyes such as walnut hulls and indigo.

Many of the same crafts were produced by African Americans, who developed their own craft traditions, often with even fewer raw materials than their white counterparts. For example, African American quilts often used patterns and colors reflective of African culture. Blacksmiths were often African American, and these skilled artisans developed both practical and decorative pieces for white and black households.

As the lifestyles of Tennesseans changed and more household items were available in stores and by mail order, crafts were produced for sale. In 1929, the Southern Highland Handicraft Guild was formed and held its first meeting in Knoxville. In 1950 the guild merged with Southern Highlanders Inc., an organization established by the Tennessee Valley Authority, and the group's marketing and promotion efforts pushed westward toward the Cumberland Plateau and Nashville.

Today, artists from around the United States have settled in Tennessee to practice modern forms of traditional crafts of quilting, weaving, pottery, furniture making, and basket making, among others. While market forces have promoted a certain false folksiness among some artists, a great many of today's practicing artisans remain true to the mountain heritage that gave birth to the craft tradition in the first place.

Music

Tennessee may be more famous for its music than for anything else. The blues was born on Beale Street; the Grand Ole Opry popularized old-time mountain music; and the Fisk Jubilee singers of Nashville introduced African American spirituals to the world. Rock 'n' roll traces its roots to Elvis Presley, Carl Perkins, Jerry Lee Lewis, and the city of Memphis.

The blues became popular in cities from New Orleans to St. Louis at the turn of the 20th century. But thanks in large part to composer and performer W. C. Handy, the musical form will be forever associated with

Memphis and Beale Street. Early blues greats like Walter "Furry" Lewis, Booker T. Washington "Bukka" White, "Little Laura" Dukes, and Ma Rainey started in Memphis.

Sun Studio recorded some of the first commercial blues records in the 1950s, but the label is most famous for discovering Elvis Presley. Stax Records created a new sound, soul, in the late 1950s and early 1960s.

Country music was born in Bristol, Tennessee, where the earliest recordings of Jimmie Rodgers and the Carter Family were made in the 1920s. In the decades that followed, Nashville became the capital of country music, beginning thanks to radio station WSM and dozens of rural musicians who trekked to town to play on the radio. America was hungry for a type of music to call its own, and country music was it. First called "hillbilly music," country was popularized by barn-dance radio shows, including the Grand Ole Opry. Over the years, country music mellowed out, adopting the Nashville sound that softened its edges and made it palatable to a wider audience. The economic impact of the music industry on Nashville approached $9.7 billion in 2015, according to the Chamber of Commerce.

In 2013, the Bureau of Labor Statistics ranked Tennessee number one in the country for its concentration of musician jobs.

Dance

Clogging, or buck dancing, is a style of folk dance that originated with the Scotch-Irish settlers in the eastern mountains of Tennessee. Characterized by an erect upper body and a fast-paced toe-heel movement with the feet, traditional clogging is improvisational. Performers move at a very fast pace to the music of string bands.

Clogging was popularized during the 1940s and 1950s on television and radio shows that showcased country music. Modern clogging is often choreographed and performed with a partner.

Clogging can trace influences from Native American and African American styles of dance as well as the traditional dance of the British Isles.

Literature

The first literature inspired by Tennessee is not well known. *The Tennessean; A Novel, Founded on Facts* is a melodramatic novel written by Anne Newport Royall and published in 1827. Its plot brings readers along on a three-day journey from Nashville to Knoxville, and it is the first novel set in Tennessee. The first novel written by a Tennessean was *Woodville; or, The Anchoret Reclaimed. A Descriptive Tale,* written by Charles W. Todd and published in Knoxville in 1832.

Later Tennessee literature is better known. English novelist **Frances Hodgson Burnett** lived in New Market and then Knoxville in the 1860s and 1870s. While best known for her tales *Little Lord Fauntleroy* and *The Secret Garden,* Burnett penned several works set in Tennessee. In the 1920s, a group of writers at Vanderbilt University emerged under the leadership of John Crowe Ransom. The group's magazine, *The Fugitive,* was published

1922-1925. The Fugitives were succeeded by the Agrarians, who published
their manifesto, *I'll Take My Stand,* in 1930. Writer **Robert Penn Warren**
was a member of both the Fugitives and the Agrarians, and he went on to
win the Pulitzer Prize for *All the King's Men,* about Governor Huey Long
of Louisiana. Warren's novels *The Cave, Flood,* and *Meet Me in the Green
Glen* are set in Tennessee.

Another award-winning Tennessee writer is **Peter Taylor,** who studied at Rhodes College and Vanderbilt University before moving to North
Carolina and writing the Pulitzer Prize-winning *A Summons to Memphis*
in 1986 and *In Tennessee Country* in 1994.

James Agee is another Pulitzer Prize winner. Raised in Knoxville, Agee
wrote poetry, journalism, and screenplays before his winning *A Death in
the Family* was published. Agee is also known for his singular work *Let Us
Now Praise Famous Men,* with photographer Walker Evans, which documented the lives of poor whites during the Great Depression.

Few people knew Memphis-born writer and historian **Shelby Foote**
until Ken Burns's landmark Civil War documentary. In addition to his
seminal trilogy on the war, Foote wrote the novel *Shiloh* in 1952.

Women have also excelled as writers in Tennessee. **Anne Armstrong**
published *The Seas of God* in 1915 and *This Day and Time* in 1930, both of
which were set in her native East Tennessee. **Evelyn Scott** wrote *The Wave,*
set during the Civil War, as well as an autobiography, *Escapade,* depicting the six years she and her common-law husband spent living in Brazil.

Perhaps the best-known female Tennessee writer is **Nikki Giovanni,**
of Knoxville, who established herself as a poet of international importance with her 1968 *Black Feeling, Black Talk.* In recent years author Ann
Patchett has built a national reputation, thanks to her articles about living
in Nashville, covering everything from the real estate to the 2010 floods.
Patchett, who wrote the acclaimed *State of Wonder* and *Bel Canto,* opened
Parnassus Books, an independent bookstore, in Nashville in 2011.

No Tennessee writer is better known or more widely acclaimed than
Alex Haley, whose *Roots* won the Pulitzer Prize and inspired a landmark
film and television series. Haley's other works include *Queen,* which is
based on the story of his grandmother, who worked and lived in Savannah,
Tennessee, on the Tennessee River.

Knoxville native **Cormac McCarthy** is widely known for his works,
including *All the Pretty Horses* and *The Road,* which were both made
into films. But McCarthy had started out writing about his native East
Tennessee in works such as *The Orchard Keeper* and *Suttree.*

Essentials

Getting There and Around

Most visitors to Tennessee drive their own cars. The highways are good, distances are manageable, and many, if not most, destinations in the state are not accessible by public transportation. Plus, the state is less than a day's drive from a large percentage of the population of the United States.

If you're coming to Memphis for a weekend getaway or a conference, you likely can manage without a car. Otherwise, you will need your own wheels to get around.

AIR

Memphis International Airport (MEM) is the main airport for flying into Memphis. There are a few smaller regional airports in the area, too, but MEM is by far the most accessible.

RAIL

Western Tennessee is easily accessible by passenger rail. Amtrak runs from Chicago to New Orleans, with stops in Memphis, Newbern-Dyersburg in West Tennessee, and Fulton on the border with Kentucky. The route, called The City of New Orleans, runs daily.

BUS

Greyhound fully serves Tennessee, with daily routes that crisscross the state in nearly every direction.

CAR

Tennessee is within one day's drive of 75 percent of the U.S. population, and most visitors to the state get here in their own cars. There are seven interstates that run into the state, from just about every direction you might want to come.

While urban centers, pit-stop motels, and population centers are all found along or very near interstates, some of Tennessee's most lovely landscapes are far from the stretches of multilane pavement (and worth the drive to get there). Because Nissan's U.S. headquarters are in Franklin, Tennessee, and because Nissan is a leader in electric cars, there are more places to pull over and charge an electric car than you might expect. Locally headquartered restaurant chain Cracker Barrel has a lot of charging stations in its parking lots.

Road Rules

Tennessee recognizes other states' driver's licenses and learner's permits. New residents are required to obtain a Tennessee license within 30 days of establishing residency, however.

Previous: old car on Beale Street; Memphis Suspension Railway to Mud Island.

Speed limits vary. On interstates limits range 55-75 miles per hour. Limits on primary and secondary routes vary based on local conditions. Travelers should pay special attention to slow zones around schools; speeding tickets in these areas often attract high penalties.

It is required by law that all drivers and passengers in a moving vehicle wear their seatbelts. Infants less than one year old must be restrained in a rear-facing car seat; children 1-3 years must be restrained in a front-facing car seat. A child of 4-8 years who is less than four feet, nine inches tall must have a booster seat.

Drunk driving is dangerous and against the law. It is illegal to drive in Tennessee with a blood alcohol concentration of 0.08 percent or more.

Car Rentals

Rental cars are widely available throughout Tennessee. The greatest concentration of rental agencies are found at major airports, but there are also neighborhood and downtown locations. Most rental agencies require the renter to be at least 24 years old; some have an even higher age requirement.

Before renting a car, call you credit card company and primary car insurance provider to find out what kind of insurance you have on a rental. You can likely forego the expensive insurance packages offered by rental companies.

For the best rates on car rentals, book early. Most companies allow you to reserve a car in advance without paying a deposit.

Taxis

Taxis are available in Memphis. Taxi stands are found in just a few locations, including airports and major tourist sites, such as Beale Street in Memphis. Otherwise you will have to call to summon a taxi.

Ride-Hailing

Ride booking services that use an app and contracted drivers in their own vehicles are becoming a popular solution in cities. **Lyft** (Lyft.com) is available in Memphis and Nashville. **Uber** (uber.com) serves Memphis, Nashville, Chattanooga, and Knoxville.

Traffic Reports

For current traffic and road reports, including weather-related closures, construction closures, and traffic jams, dial 511 from any mobile or landline phone. You can also log on to www.tn511.com.

RECREATIONAL VEHICLES

Recreational vehicles are an increasingly popular way to see Tennessee due to the prevalence of good campgrounds and the beautiful landscape of the state.

All state park campgrounds welcome RVs and provide utilities such as water, electricity, and a dump station. For people who enjoy the outdoors but do not want to forgo the basic comforts of home, RVs provide some real advantages. RVs range from little trailers that pop up to provide space for sleeping to monstrous homes on wheels. Gas mileage ranges 7-13 miles per gallon, depending on the size and age of the RV.

All RVers should have mercy on other drivers and pull over from time to time so that traffic can pass, especially on mountain roads that are steep and difficult for RVs to climb.

RV Rentals

You can rent an RV for a one-way or local trip from **Cruise America** (www.cruiseamerica.com), which has locations in Knoxville (6100 Western Ave., 865/450-5009), Nashville (201 Donelson Pk., 615/885-4281), and Memphis (10230 Hwy. 70, Lakeland, 901/867-0039). Renters should be 25 years or older. Rental rates vary depending on the size of the vehicle and other factors. They also charge for mileage, and you can buy kits that include sheets, towels, dishes, and other basic necessities.

Recreation

STATE PARKS

Tennessee's state parks are glorious and one of the state's best calling cards. The state has 54 parks and 77 state natural areas, stretching from the Appalachian Mountains in the east to the banks of the Mississippi River in the west. State parks and natural areas encompass 185,000 acres throughout the state. In 2007, Tennessee's parks were judged the best in the nation by the National Recreation and Park Association. The commendation came after a long and bitter fight over user fees and state budget woes that led to the closure of 14 parks and the imposition of user fees at 23 parks between 2002 and 2006. The fight over the future of the state parks illustrated how valuable they are indeed; none of the parks have entrances fees.

Each state park includes basic amenities such as picnic facilities and day-use areas with public restrooms, water, and a park office of some kind. Most parks also have campgrounds, hiking trails, playgrounds, and facilities for sports such as volleyball, basketball, and baseball. A number of parks have swimming beaches, bicycle trails, areas for fishing or hunting, and backcountry campsites.

The park system includes 6 parks with inns, 12 with golf courses (and 2 disc golf sources), 8 with restaurants, and 4 with marinas for motorized boats. A number of parks also have cabins, ideal for families or other groups.

For travelers who enjoy the out-of-doors, the state parks are some of the best places in the state to visit. Despite persistent budget problems, the parks are generally well maintained. Accommodations are not luxurious, but they are clean and comfortable, and the natural beauty that exists in many of the parks is unparalleled. Camping in a state park sure beats the KOA any day.

Detailed information about fees, amenities, and services may be found on the state park website (http://state.tn.us/environment/parks). You can also request a published map and brochure. Enthusiasts may also want to subscribe to the *Tennessee Conservationist,* a magazine published by the State Department of Environment and Conservation.

HIKING

Opportunities to hike are abundant in Tennessee. State parks, national forests, national parks, and wildlife refuges are just a few of the areas where you will find places for a walk in the woods.

High-profile hiking trails such as the Appalachian Trail in the eastern mountains are indeed special. But lesser-known walks are often equally spectacular, and the best hike may well be the one closest to where you are right now.

Day hikes require just a few pieces of gear: comfortable and sturdy shoes; a day pack with water, food, and a map; and several layers of clothing, especially during volatile spring and fall months. In the winter, it's a good idea to bring a change of socks and extra layers of warm clothes.

Other gear is optional: A walking stick makes rough or steep terrain a bit easier, and a camera is always a nice idea.

Whenever you go hiking, tell someone where you're going and when you expect to be back. Do not expect cell phones to work on the trail.

Many state parks and the national parks in the eastern mountains welcome overnight hikers. Backpackers must carry lightweight tents, sleeping bags, food, and extra gear on their backs. They must also register in advance. You can sometimes reserve backcountry campsites. These campsites offer little more than a clearing for your tent and a ring of stones for your fire. Some are built near sources of water. Some trails have overnight shelters, especially nice in winter.

Hiking is one of the best ways to experience Tennessee's nature, and there are few better ways to spend a day or two.

BICYCLING

Bicycling is an increasingly popular pastime in Tennessee. Only in a handful of urban areas, and on some college campuses, is bicycling a form of regular transportation. But mountain and road biking is popular for staying fit and having fun. Many area parks offer BMX tracks.

Of course you can bicycle just about anywhere (but not on the interstates). Cities such as Nashville, Chattanooga, Knoxville, and Murfreesboro have greenways especially for bikers (and walkers). Dedicated mountain bike trails are popping up in parks across the state, including at Montgomery Bell State Park, Big Ridge State Park, and Meeman-Shelby Forest State Park. City parks in Memphis and Nashville also welcome bikers.

The **Tennessee Bicycle Racing Association** (www.tbra.org) promotes
biking and is an umbrella organization for several local bike groups. The
Tennessee Mountain Biking Alliance (www.mtbtn.org) promotes mountain
biking and can put you in touch with mountain bikers in your neck of the
woods. Local bike shops are also a good place to find out about good bike
routes, local safety issues, and upcoming events.

Accommodations

HOTELS AND MOTELS

Chain motels are ubiquitous, particularly along interstates. These properties are entirely predictable; their amenities depend on the price tag and
location. Most motel chains allow you to make reservations in advance by
telephone or on the Internet. Most motels require a credit card number at
the time of reservation, but they don't usually charge your card until you
arrive. Always ask about the cancellation policy to avoid paying for a room
that you do not ultimately need or use.

Savvy shoppers can save money on their hotel room. Shop around, and
pay attention to price differentials based on location; if you're willing to be
a few miles up the interstate from the city, you'll realize some significant
savings. You may also be amazed by the power of the words "That rate
seems high to me. Do you have anything better?" Employed regularly, this
approach will usually save you a few bucks each night, at least.

Chain motels do not offer unique accommodations, and only the rarest
among them is situated somewhere more charming than an asphalt parking lot. But for travelers who are looking for flexibility, familiarity, and a
good deal, chain motels can fit the bill.

Independent motels and hotels range from no-brand roadside motels to
upscale boutique hotels in urban centers. By their very nature, these properties are each a little different. Boutique hotels tend to be more expensive
than chain hotels, but they also allow you to feel as if you are staying in a
place with a history and character of its own. They may also offer person-
alized service that is not available at cookie-cutter motels.

BED-AND-BREAKFASTS

Bed-and-breakfasts are about as far from a chain motel as one can get.
Usually located in small towns, rural areas, and quiet residential neighborhoods of major cities, bed-and-breakfasts are independent guesthouses.
The quality of the offering depends entirely on the hosts, and the entire
bed-and-breakfast experience often takes on the character and tone of the
person in whose home you are sleeping. Good bed-and-breakfast hosts can
sense the line between being welcoming and overly chatty, but some seem
to struggle with this.

Bed-and-breakfasts offer a number of advantages over the typical motel.
Their locations are often superior, the guest rooms have lots of character

and charm, and a full and often homemade breakfast is included. Some bed-and-breakfasts are located in historic buildings, and many are furnished with antiques.

Reservations for bed-and-breakfasts are not as flexible as most motels. Many bed-and-breakfasts require a deposit, and many require payment in full before you arrive. Making payments can be a challenge, too; while some are equipped to process credit cards, others accept only checks and cash. Cancellation policies are also more stringent than most motels. All of this can make it hard for travelers who like to be flexible and leave things till the last minute. Additionally, if you're bringing children with you, be sure to check that your bed-and-breakfast allows children; some don't. If your travel plans are certain and you just can't bear another night in a bland hotel room, a bed-and-breakfast is the ideal alternative.

Bed-and-breakfast rates vary but generally range $90-150 per night based on double occupancy.

Bed and Breakfast Inns Online (www.bbonline.com) is a national listing service that includes a number of Tennessee bed-and-breakfasts.

PRIVATE RESIDENCES

Websites aggregators like **Vacation Rental By Owner** (vrbo.com) and **Airbnb** (airbnb.com) have become a popular way to find a room, apartment, or house to rent. Accommodations may be less expensive that traditional lodging, and often include parking and kitchens. You have fewer recourses if something goes wrong, however, so ask questions before you book.

Food

Throughout Tennessee, you will find restaurants that specialize in local and regional dishes. In urban centers, there is a wide variety of dining available, from international eateries to fine-dining restaurants.

Chain restaurants, including fast-food joints, are all over the state. But travelers owe it to themselves to eat in local restaurants for a taste of something more authentic.

MEAT-AND-THREES

Meat-and-threes, also called plate-lunch diners, are found throughout Tennessee, with the greatest concentration in Memphis and Nashville. The name is used to refer to the type of restaurant and the meal itself. These eateries serve the type of food that Tennesseans once cooked at home: main dish meats like baked chicken, meat loaf, fried catfish, and chicken and dumplings; side dishes (also called "vegetables"), including macaroni and cheese, mashed potatoes, greens, creamed corn, squash, and fried okra; breads, including corn bread, biscuits, and yeast rolls; and desserts like peach cobbler, Jell-O, and cream pies. Hands down, these diners are the best home cooking.

Plate-lunch diners focus on the midday meal. Most offer a different menu of meats and sides daily. Large restaurants may have as many as eight different main dishes to choose from; smaller diners may offer two or three. Some are set up cafeteria-style, and others employ servers. All offer a good value for the money and generally speedy food service.

Meat-and-threes exist in rural and urban communities, although in the countryside there's less fuss attached. They are simply where people go to eat.

The food served in these restaurants is generally hearty; health-conscious eaters should be careful. Vegetarians should also note that most vegetable dishes, like greens, are often cooked with meat.

REGIONAL SPECIALTIES
Barbecue

Memphis is the epicenter of Tennessee's barbecue culture. Here is hosted an annual festival dedicated to barbecue, and bona fide barbecue pits burn daily. In Memphis, they'll douse anything with barbecue sauce, hence the city's specialty: barbecue spaghetti.

Barbecue restaurants are usually humble places by appearances, with characters behind the counter and in the kitchen. Most swear by their own special barbecue recipe and guard it jealously. Nearly all good barbecue, however, requires time and patience, as the meat—usually pork—is smoked for hours and sometimes days over a fire. After the meat is cooked, it is tender and juicy and doused with barbecue sauce, which is tangy and sweet.

Pork barbecue is the most common, and it's often served pulled next to soft white bread. Barbecue chicken, turkey, ribs, bologna, and beef can also be found on many menus.

The Southern Foodways Alliance (SFA), part of the University of Mississippi's Center for the Study of Southern Culture, conducted an oral history project about Memphis and West Tennessee barbecue in the early 2000s. You can read transcripts of the interviews and see photos on the SFA website at www.southernfoodways.com.

Catfish

Fried catfish is a food tradition that started along Tennessee's rivers, where river catfish are caught. Today, fried catfish served in restaurants is just as likely to come from a catfish farm. For real river catfish, look for restaurants located near rivers and lakes, such as those near Reelfoot Lake in northwestern Tennessee, or the City Fish Market in Brownsville.

Fried catfish (it's rarely served any way besides fried) is normally coated with a thin dusting of cornmeal, seasonings, and flour. On its own, the fish is relatively bland. Tangy tartar sauce, vinegar-based hot sauce, and traditional sides like coleslaw and baked beans enliven the flavor. Hush puppies are the traditional accompaniment.

FARMERS MARKETS

Farmers markets are popping up in more and more Tennessee communities. Knoxville, Nashville, Oak Ridge, and Memphis have large markets every Saturday (Nashville's operates daily). Dozens of small towns and neighborhoods have their own weekly, seasonal markets.

There is a great deal of variety when it comes to the types of markets that exist. Some markets take place under tents, provide entertainment, and invite artisans to sell arts and crafts as well as food products. Other markets consist of little more than a bunch of farmers who have arranged the week's harvest on the back of their tailgates.

Regardless of the style, farmers markets are a great place to meet people and buy wholesome food.

The State Department of Agriculture (www.agriculture.state.tn.us) maintains a listing of all registered farmers markets, including locations and contact information.

Travel Tips

OPPORTUNITIES FOR STUDY

Tennessee is home to almost 50 colleges and universities, plus 13 public community colleges. The University of Tennessee, with campuses in Knoxville, Chattanooga, and Martin, is the largest. Other public colleges and universities include East Tennessee State University in Johnson City, Middle Tennessee State University in Murfreesboro, Tennessee State University in Nashville, and the University of Memphis. Private colleges include the historically black Fisk University in Nashville and Lemoyne-Owen College in Memphis; the University of the South at Sewanee, which is affiliated with the Episcopal Church; Memphis College of Art and Rhodes College in Memphis; and Vanderbilt University in Nashville. Each of these, plus the 31 other private institutions of higher learning, offer myriad short- and long-term education programs in fields as various as religious studies and medicine.

WOMEN TRAVELING ALONE

Women traveling alone in Tennessee may encounter a few people who don't understand why, but most people will simply leave you alone. Solo women might find themselves the object of unwanted attention, especially at bars and restaurants at night. But usually a firm "I'm not interested" will do the trick.

GAY AND LESBIAN TRAVELERS

Tennessee's gay, lesbian, bisexual, and transgender people have a mixed bag. On one hand, this is the Bible Belt, a state where not long ago a bill was introduced that would have banned teachers from even saying the word *gay* in the classroom. (This is often referred to as the "Don't Say Gay" bill.) On the other hand, there has been no better time to be gay in Tennessee. More and more social, civic, and political organizations are waking up to the gay community, and there are vibrant gay scenes in many Tennessee cities.

For gay travelers, this means that the experience on the road can vary tremendously. You may or may not be able to expect a warm welcome at the mom-and-pop diner out in the country, but you can find good gay nightlife and gay-friendly lodging in many cities.

The decision about how out to be on the road is entirely up to you, but be prepared for some harassment if you are open everywhere you go. The farther off the beaten track you travel, the less likely it is that the people you encounter have had many opportunities to get to know openly gay people. Some may be downright mean, but others probably won't even notice.

Several specific guidebooks and websites give helpful listings of gay-friendly hotels, restaurants, and bars. The Damron guides (www.damron.com) offer Tennessee listings; the International Gay and Lesbian Travel Association (IGLTA, www.iglta.org) is a trade organization with listings of gay-friendly hotels, tour operators, and much more. San Francisco-based Now, Voyager (www.nowvoyager.com) is a gay-owned and gay-operated travel agency that specializes in gay tours, vacation packages, and cruises.

You should also check out local gay and lesbian organizations and newspapers. The **Memphis Gay and Lesbian Community Center** (892 S. Cooper St., 901/278-6422, www.mglcc.org) is a clearinghouse of information for the gay and lesbian community. It has a directory of gay-friendly businesses, host social events, and promote tolerance and equality.

Mid-South Pride (www.midsouthpride.org) organizes Memphis Pride in June.

SENIOR TRAVELERS

Elderhostel (800/454-5768, www.elderhostel.org), which organizes educational tours for people over 55, offers tours in Memphis and Nashville.

For discounts and help with trip planning, try the **AARP** (800/687-2277, www.aarp.org), which offers a full-service travel agency, trip insurance, a motor club, and AARP Passport program, which provides you with senior discounts for hotels, car rentals, and other things.

Persons over 55 should always check for a senior citizen discount. Most attractions and some hotels and restaurants have special pricing for senior citizens.

TRAVELERS WITH DISABILITIES

More people with disabilities are traveling than ever before. The Americans with Disabilities Act requires most public buildings to make provisions for disabled people, although in practice accessibility may be spotty.

When you make your hotel reservations, always check that the hotel is prepared to accommodate you. Airlines will also make special arrangements for you if you request help in advance. To reduce stress, try to travel during off-peak times.

Several national organizations have information and advice about traveling with disabilities. **The Society for Accessible Travel and Hospitality** (www.sath.org) publishes links to major airlines' accessibility policies and publishes travel tips for people with all types of disabilities, including blindness, deafness, mobility disorders, diabetes, kidney disease, and arthritis. The society publishes *Open World,* a magazine about accessible travel.

Wheelchair Getaways (800/642-2042, www.wheelchairgetaways.com) is a national chain specializing in renting vans that are wheelchair accessible or otherwise designed for disabled drivers and travelers. Wheelchair Getaways has locations in Memphis (901/795-6533 or 866/762-165), and it will deliver to other locations in the state.

Avis offers **Avis Access,** a program for travelers with disabilities. Call the dedicated 24-hour toll-free number (888/879-4273) for help renting a car with features such as transfer boards, hand controls, spinner knobs, and swivel seats.

TRAVELING WITH CHILDREN

It is hard to imagine a state better suited for family vacations than Tennessee. The state parks provide numerous places to camp, hike, swim, fish, and explore, and cities have attractions like zoos, children's museums, aquariums, and trains.

Many hotels and inns offer special discounts for families, and casual restaurants almost always have a children's menu with lower-priced, kid-friendly choices.

FOREIGN TRAVELERS

Tennessee attracts a fair number of foreign visitors. Elvis, the international popularity of blues and country music, and the beauty of the eastern mountains bring people to the state from all over the globe.

Communication

Foreign travelers will find a warm welcome. Those in the tourist trade are used to dealing with all sorts of people and will be pleased that you have come from so far away to visit their home. If you are not a native English speaker, it may be difficult to understand the local accent at first. Just smile and ask the person to say it again, a bit slower. Good humor and a positive attitude will help at all times.

Visas and Officialdom

Most citizens of a foreign country require a visa to enter the United States. There are many types of visas, issued according to the purpose of your visit. Business and pleasure travelers apply for B-1 and B-2 visas, respectively.

When you apply for your visa, you will be required to prove that the purpose of your trip is business, pleasure, or for medical treatment; that you plan to remain in the United States for a limited period; and that you have a place of residence outside the United States. Apply for your visa at the nearest U.S. embassy. For more information, contact the U.S. Citizenship and Immigration Service (www.uscis.gov).

Nationals of 38 countries may be able to use the Visa Waiver Program, operated by Customs and Border Protection. Presently, these 38 countries are: Andorra, Australia, Austria, Belgium, Brunei, Chile, Czech Republic, Denmark (including Greenland and Faroe Islands), Estonia, Finland, France, Germany, Greece, Hungary, Iceland, Ireland, Italy, Japan, Latvia, Liechtenstein, Lithuania, Luxembourg, Malta, Monaco, the Netherlands (including Aruba, Bonaire, Curacao, Saba, and Sint Maarten), New Zealand, Norway, Portugal (including Azores and Madeira), San Marino, South Korea, Singapore, Slovakia, Slovenia, South Korea, Spain, Sweden, Switzerland, Taiwan, and the United Kingdom.

Take note that in recent years the United States has begun to require visa-waiver participants to have upgraded passports with digital photographs and machine-readable information. They have also introduced requirements that even visa-waiver citizens register in advance before arriving in the United States. For more information about the Visa Waiver Program, contact the Customs and Border Protection Agency (www.travel.state.gov).

All foreign travelers are now required to participate in U.S. Visit, a program operated by the Department of Homeland Security. Under the program, your fingerprints and photograph are taken—digitally and without ink—as you are being screened by the immigration officer.

Arrival

The Memphis airport is well equipped for foreign travelers. The lone international airline, Northwest/KLM Royal Dutch Airlines, provides interpreters for the Customs Clearance Facility and the boarding areas for international flights. It can accommodate Dutch-, German-, Arabic-, Spanish-, and French-speaking passengers.

International travel services are provided at the Business Service Center (Ticket Lobby B, 901/922-8090, 7am-7:30pm Mon.-Fri., 10am-7:30pm Sat., 11am-7:30pm Sun.). Here you can exchange currency, buy travel insurance, make telephone calls and send faxes, wire money, and buy traveler's checks. An additional kiosk is located in Concourse B near the international gates (gate B-36). Here you can buy travel insurance and exchange currency. The hours are 4:30pm-7:30pm daily.

Memphis International Airport is a "Transit Without Visa" port of entry. This means that foreign travelers whose flight will connect through Memphis on the way to another foreign destination beyond the United States no longer need a U.S. transit visa just to connect.

Health and Safety

DISEASES
West Nile Virus

West Nile virus was first recorded in humans in the United States in the early 2000s, and by 2007 nearly every state, including Tennessee, had reported confirmed cases of the disease. West Nile is spread by mosquitoes.

Summer is mosquito season in Tennessee. You can prevent mosquito breeding by eliminating standing water around your property. You can prevent mosquito bites by wearing an insect repellant containing 30-50 percent DEET. An alternative to DEET, picaridin, is available in 7 and 15 percent concentrations and would need to be applied more frequently. Wearing long-sleeved pants and shirts and not being outdoors during dusk and dawn are also ways to avoid exposure to mosquitoes.

Fever, chills, weakness, drowsiness, and fatigue are some of the symptoms of West Nile virus.

Lyme Disease

Lyme disease is a bacterial infection spread by deer ticks. The first indication you might have Lyme disease is the appearance of a red rash where you have been bitten by a tick. Following that, symptoms are flu-like. During late-stage Lyme disease, neurological effects are reported.

Ticks are external parasites that attach themselves to warm-blooded creatures like dogs, deer, and humans. Ticks suck blood from their host.

Tick bites are unpleasant enough, even if there is no infection of Lyme disease. After coming in from the woods, especially if you were walking off-trail, carefully inspect your body for ticks. If one has attached itself to you, remove it by carefully "unscrewing" it from your body with tweezers.

You can avoid ticks by wearing long sleeves and pants, tucking in your shirt, and wearing a hat. You can minimize your exposure to ticks by staying on trails and walking paths where you don't brush up against trees and branches.

White-Nose Syndrome

In 2006 in upstate New York, a caver noticed a substance on the noses of hibernating bats, as well as a few dead bats. The next year, more of both were found. Now bats dying of a fungus called "white-nose syndrome" have been found as far south as Tennessee.

Researchers are still trying to find out what causes the deadly (to bats, not people) fungus. Until then, certain caves may be closed to prevent the disease from spreading. Check individual cave listings before heading out.

Poison Ivy

If there is one plant that you should learn to identify, it is poison ivy. This woody vine grows in woods all around Tennessee. Touching it can leave you with a painful and terribly uncomfortable reaction.

Poison ivy is green, and the leaves grow in clusters of three. There are no thorns. Its berries are a gray-white color, and if the vine is climbing, you will notice root "hairs" on the vine. The following mnemonic might help: "Leaves of three, let it be; berries white, danger in sight."

An estimated 15-35 percent of people are not allergic to poison ivy. But after repeated exposure this protection is worn down. People who are allergic will experience more and more severe reactions with each episode of exposure.

Poison ivy is easily spread over your body by your hands, or from person to person through skin-to-skin contact. Never touch your eyes or face if you think you may have touched poison ivy, and always wash yourself with hot soapy water if you think you may have come into contact with the vine.

Treat poison ivy rashes with over-the-counter itch creams. In severe cases, you may need to go to the doctor.

VENOMOUS SNAKES

The vast majority of snakes in Tennessee are nonvenomous. Only four species of venomous snakes exist there. Copperheads (northern and southern) live throughout the state, along with the timber rattlesnake. The pygmy rattlesnake lives in the Kentucky Lake region, and the cottonmouth water moccasin is found in wet areas in the western part of the state.

Venomous snakes of Tennessee can usually by identified by their elliptical (cat-eye) shaped pupils (not that you really want to get close enough to see that). Most also have thick bodies, blunt tails, and triangular-shaped heads.

MEDICAL SERVICES

Hospitals, medical centers, and doctors' offices are located throughout the state. Walk-in medical centers may be found in the yellow pages and are the best bet for minor needs while you're on vacation. In an emergency, proceed to the closest hospital or call 911.

The single most important thing you can have if you get sick while traveling is health insurance. Before you leave, check with your insurance provider about in-network doctors and medical facilities in the area where you'll be traveling.

Prescriptions

Always travel with your prescription drugs in their original container and with a copy of the prescription issued by your doctor. If you can, get refills before you leave. National chains of many drugstores exist across the state.

DRUGS

Tennessee's greatest drug problem is with methamphetamine, the highly addictive stimulant sometimes called "speed," "crank," and "ice," among other names. During the 1990s and 2000s, meth use spread quickly through rural America, including Tennessee. In 2004, Tennessee passed comprehensive legislation to combat meth. A year later, some 60 percent of Tennessee counties reported that meth remained their most serious drug problem.

The state's anti-meth strategy has been to aggressively seek out illegal meth labs, increase public education about meth use, and promote recovery programs. Despite the efforts, it is still difficult to eliminate meth use, partly because meth is relatively easy to manufacture in so-called labs, which can be built in homes, hotel rooms, trailers, and even vehicles.

Meth is a dangerous and highly addictive drug. It takes a terrible toll on the health of users, creates myriad family and social problems, and is among one of the most addictive drugs out there.

CRIME

Crime is a part of life anywhere, and travelers should take precautions to avoid being a victim of crime. Leave valuables at home and secure your hotel room and car at all times (including GPS devices, tablets, and other car-friendly technology). Always be aware of your surroundings, and don't allow yourself to be drawn into conversations with strangers in deserted, dark, or otherwise sketchy areas. Single travelers, especially women, should take special care to stay in well-lit and highly populated areas, especially at night.

Information and Services

MONEY
Banks

Dozens of local and regional banks are found throughout Tennessee. Most banks will cash traveler's checks, exchange currency, and send wire transfers. Banks are generally open weekdays 9am-4pm, although some are open later and on Saturday. Automatic teller machines (ATMs) are ubiquitous at grocery stores, live-music venues, and elsewhere, and many are compatible with bank cards bearing the Plus or Cirrus icons. Between fees charged by your own bank and the bank that owns the ATM you are using, expect to pay $2-5 extra to get cash from an ATM that does not belong to your own bank.

Sales Tax

Sales tax is charged on all goods, including food and groceries.

The sales tax you pay is split between the state and local governments. Tennessee's sales tax is 5 percent on food and groceries and 7 percent on all other goods. Cities and towns add an additional "local use tax" of 1.5-2.75 percent, making the tax as high as 9.25 percent in Nashville, Memphis, Knoxville, and Chattanooga.

Hotel Tax

There is no statewide tax on hotel rooms, but 45 different cities have established their own hotel tax, ranging 5-7 percent.

Cost

Tennessee routinely ranks favorably on cost-of-living indexes. Visitors can comfortably eat their fill in casual restaurants and coffee shops for $35 a day, although it is possible to spend much more if you prefer to eat in upscale restaurants.

The cost of accommodations varies widely, depending on the area you are visiting, the type of accommodations you are seeking, and when you are traveling. The most expensive hotel rooms are in urban centers. Rates go up during major events, on weekends, and during peak travel months in the summer. Cheaper accommodations will be found on the outskirts of town and along rural interstate routes. Budget travelers should consider camping.

If you are not coming in your own car, one of your most substantial expenses will be a rental car. Most rentals bottom out at $35 a day, and rates can be much higher if you don't reserve in advance or if you are renting only for a day or two.

Discounts

Most historic sites, museums, and attractions offer special discounts for senior citizens and children under 12. Some attractions also have discounts for students and members of the military. Even if you don't see any discount posted, it is worth asking if one exists.

Many chain hotels offer discounts for AAA members.

Bargaining

Consumer Reports magazine reported that you can often get a better hotel rate simply by asking for one. If the rate you are quoted sounds a little high, simply say that it is more than you were planning to spend and ask if it can offer a better rate. Many times, especially out of season, the answer will be yes. Your negotiations will be more successful if you are willing to walk away if the answer is no.

Tipping

You should tip waiters and waitresses 15-20 percent in a sit-down restaurant. You can tip 5-10 percent in a cafeteria or restaurant where you collect your own food from the counter.

Tip a bellhop or bag handler $1 per bag, or more if they went out of their way to help you.

TOURIST INFORMATION

The **Tennessee Department of Tourism Development** (615/741-2159, www.tnvacation.com) is a source of visitor information about Tennessee.

It publishes an annual guide that contains hotel and attraction listings. The website has lots of links to local attractions and chambers of commerce.

Many cities have their own tourist organizations: Memphis, Nashville, Knoxville, Chattanooga, and Clarksville are among the Tennessee cities with a visitors bureau. Specific listings for visitor information are found throughout this book.

In West Tennessee there is the **Southwest Tennessee Tourism Association** (www.tast.tn.org) and the **Northwest Tennessee Tourism Association** (www.reelfootlakeoutdoors.com).

If all else fails, contact the chamber of commerce for the county you will be visiting. Chambers of commerce will willingly mail you a sheaf of brochures and any visitor information that may exist. If you are already in town, stop by in person. You are sure to find someone who will be glad to help you.

Maps

Rand McNally publishes the best maps of Tennessee. In addition to the statewide map, Rand McNally publishes maps of Memphis, Nashville, Knoxville, Chattanooga, the Great Smoky Mountains National Park, Clarksville, Murfreesboro-Smyrna, and Gatlinburg-Pigeon Forge. You can buy Rand McNally maps from bookstores and through online sales outlets like Amazon.com. Rand McNally also sells downloadable PDF maps that you can view on your computer or print out.

For trail maps or topographical maps of parks and other natural areas, look for National Geographic's Trails Illustrated series.

The State Department of Transportation updates its official transportation map annually. Request a free copy at www.tdot.state.tn.us or by calling 615/741-2848. The official map is also available from many Tennessee welcome centers, chambers of commerce, and other tourism-related offices.

The state also creates maps of dozens of Tennessee cities and towns. All these maps are available for free download from the department of transportation website.

Many GPS apps are now available for smartphones and other smart devices.

COMMUNICATION
Area Codes

Tennessee has seven different area codes, but Memphis and vicinity use 901.

Cell Phones

Cell phone signals are powerful and reliable in cities and along the interstates. In rural parts of the state you should not count on your cell phone, and in mountainous areas, such as the Cumberland Plateau and the Great Smoky Mountains National Park, forget about it altogether.

The eastern third of Tennessee lies in the Eastern time zone; Middle and West Tennessee are in the Central time zone, one hour earlier. The time zone line runs a slanted course from Signal Mountain in the south to the Big South Fork National River and Recreation Area in the north. The time zone line falls at mile marker 340 along I-40, just west of Rockwood and a few miles east of Crossville. Chattanooga, Dayton, Rockwood, Crossville, Rugby, Fall Creek Falls State Park, the Catoosa Wildlife Management Area, and Big South Fork lie close to or on the time zone line, and visitors to these areas should take special care to ensure they are on the right clock.

ESSENTIALS
INFORMATION AND SERVICES

Resources

Suggested Reading

GENERAL HISTORY

Bergeron, Paul H. *Paths of the Past: Tennessee, 1770-1970.* Knoxville: University of Tennessee Press, 1979. This is a concise, straight-up history of Tennessee with a few illustrations and maps.

Corlew, Robert E. *Tennessee: A Short History.* Knoxville: University of Tennessee Press, 1990. The definitive survey of Tennessee history, this text was first written in 1969 and has been updated several times by writers, including Stanley J. Folmsbee and Enoch Mitchell. This is a useful reference guide for a serious reader.

Dykeman, Wilma. *Tennessee.* New York: W. W. Norton & Company and the American Association for State and Local History, 1984. Novelist and essayist Dykeman says more about the people of Tennessee and the events that shaped the modern state in this slim and highly readable volume than you would find in the most detailed and plodding historical account. It becomes a companion and a means through which to understand the Tennessee spirit and character.

SPECIALIZED HISTORY

Beifuss, Joan Turner. *At the River I Stand.* Brooklyn NY: Carlson Pub., 1985. This account of the Memphis garbage men's strike of 1968 is told from the ground up. It places the assassination of Dr. Martin Luther King Jr. in its immediate, if not historical, context.

Bond, Beverley G., and Janann Sherman. *Memphis: In Black and White.* Mount Pleasant SC: Arcadia Publishing, 2003. This lively history of Memphis pays special attention to the dynamics of race and class. The slim and easy-to-read volume contains interesting anecdotes and lots of illustrations. It is an excellent introduction to the city.

Branch, Taylor. *Parting the Waters: America in the King Years 1954-63.* New York: Simon and Schuster, 1989. The most authoritative account of the civil rights movement, told through the life of Dr. Martin Luther King Jr. The first in a three-volume account of the movement, *Parting the Waters* includes

Egerton, John. *Speak Now Against the Day: The Generation Before the Civil Rights Movement in the South.* Chapel Hill: University of North Carolina Press, 1995. Egerton tells the relatively unacknowledged story of Southerners, white and black, who stood up against segregation and racial hatred during the years before the civil rights movement.

Honey, Michael. *Going Down Jericho Road: The Memphis Strike, Martin Luther King's Last Campaign.* New York: W. W. Norton & Co., 2007. Labor historian Honey depicts with academic detail and novelistic drama the Memphis Sanitation Strike of 1968. He documents Memphis of the late 1960s and the quest for economic justice that brought Dr. King to the city. King's assassination and its aftermath are depicted in devastating detail.

Potter, Jerry O. *Sultana Tragedy: America's Greatest Maritime Disaster.* Gretna LA: Pelican Publishing Company, 1992. The definitive account of American's worst maritime disaster. The end of the Civil War and the assassination of Abraham Lincoln grabbed the headlines in April 1864, so much so that the sinking of the *Sultana* and the death of more than 1,800 men in the Mississippi River near Memphis went almost unnoticed. This book tells a tale more poignant and moving than the loss of the *Titanic*.

Sides, Hampton. *Hellhound on His Trail: The Stalking of Martin Luther King, Jr. and the International Hunt for His Assassin.* New York: Doubleday, 2004. A well-written, captivating account of MLK's murder and the efforts to nab his killer. Sides provides perspective on Memphis's troubled history.

Sword, Wiley. *The Confederacy's Last Hurrah: Spring Hill, Franklin and Nashville.* Lawrence: University Press of Kansas, 2004. This is a well-written and devastating account of John Bell Hood's disastrous campaign through Middle Tennessee during the waning months of the Confederacy. It was a campaign that cost the South more than 23,000 men. With unflinching honesty, Sword describes the opportunities lost and poor decisions made by General Hood.

BIOGRAPHY

James, Marquis. *The Raven: A Biography of Sam Houston.* Indianapolis: The Bobbs-Merrill Company, 1929. Possibly the most remarkable Tennessean in history, Sam Houston was raised by the Cherokee, memorized Homer's *Iliad,* and was twice elected governor of Tennessee before he headed west to the new American frontier to become president of the Texas Republic.

Leeming, David. *Amazing Grace: A Life of Beauford Delaney.* New York: Oxford University Press (USA), 1998. Beauford Delaney was a brilliant but often overlooked modernist painter who was born in Knoxville in 1901. African American and gay, Delaney later moved to New York, where he worked as an artist and moved in circles that included James Baldwin and Henry Miller.

Moore, Carmen. *Somebody's Angel Child: The Story of Bessie Smith.* New York: Thomas Cromwell Company, 1969. The illustrated story of Chattanooga native Bessie Smith's remarkable rise to, then fall from, the top of the music world.

MUSIC

Carlin, Richard. *Country Music.* New York: Black Dog and Leventhal Publishers, 2006. This is a highly illustrated, well-written, and useful reference for fans of country music. It profiles the people, places, and events that contributed to country's evolution. With lots of graphic elements and photographs, it is a good book to dip into.

Gordon, Robert. *It Came from Memphis.* Boston: Faber and Faber, 1994. Memphis resident Gordon takes the back roads to tell the remarkable musical story that emerged from Memphis during the 1950s and 1960s. He paints a textured picture of the milieu from which rock 'n' roll eventually rose.

Guralnick, Peter. *Careless Love: The Unmaking of Elvis Presley.* Boston: Little, Brown and Company, 1999. Volume two of Guralnick's definitive biography of Elvis Presley. Guralnick writes in the introduction that he "knows of no sadder story" than Presley's life from 1958 until his death in 1977. The book unflinchingly examines the gradual unraveling of America's greatest pop star.

Guralnick, Peter. *Last Train to Memphis: The Rise of Elvis Presley.* Boston: Little, Brown and Company, 1994. Quite possibly the definitive biography of the King. In volume one, Guralnick re-creates Presley's first 24 years, including his childhood in Mississippi and Tennessee, his remarkable rise to fame, and the pivotal events of 1958, when he was drafted into the army and buried his beloved mother.

Handy, W. C. *Father of the Blues.* New York: The Macmillan Company, 1941. This memoir by Memphis's most famous blues man depicts the city during the first quarter of the 20th century. It is an entertaining and endearing read.

Kingsbury, Paul, ed. *Will the Circle Be Unbroken: Country Music in America.* London: DK Adult, 2006. An illustrated collection of articles by 43 writers, including several performing artists, this book is a useful reference on the genre's development from 1920 until the present.

Raichelson, Richard M. *Beale Street Talks: A Walking Tour Down the Home of the Blues*. Memphis: Arcadia Records, 1999. A slim, well-written book that describes Beale Street as it was and Beale Street as it is. This is a handy companion for exploring the street.

Sharp, Tim. *Memphis Music: Before the Blues*. Mount Pleasant SC: Arcadia Publishing, 2007. Part of the Images of America series, this work includes rare and evocative photographs of Memphis people. The result is a painting of the backdrop on which the Memphis blues were born in the early 20th century.

Wolfe, Charles K. *Tennessee Strings*. Knoxville: University of Tennessee Press, 1977. The definitive survey of Tennessee musical history. This slim volume is easy to read.

Zimmerman, Peter Coats. *Tennessee Music: Its People and Places*. San Francisco: Miller Freeman Books, 1998. Tries, and succeeds, to do the impossible: tell the varied stories of Tennessee music all the way from Bristol to Memphis. Nicely illustrated.

REFERENCE

Van West, Carroll, ed. *The Tennessee Encyclopedia of History and Culture*. Nashville: Tennessee Historical Society and Rutledge Hill Press, 1998. Perhaps the most valuable tome on Tennessee, this 1,200-page encyclopedia covers the people, places, events, and movements that defined Tennessee history and the culture of its people. Dip in frequently, and you will be all the wiser.

FICTION

Burton, Linda, ed. *Stories from Tennessee*. Knoxville: University of Tennessee Press, 1983. An anthology of Tennessee literature, the volume begins with a story by David Crockett on hunting in Tennessee and concludes with works by 20th-century authors such as Shelby Foote, Cormac McCarthy, and Robert Drake.

Grisham, John. *The Firm*. Boston: G. K. Hall, 1992. Probably the most celebrated Memphis-set novel in recent years, especially following the success of the eponymous film. Mitchell McDeere takes on corrupt and criminal mob lawyers. It includes references to many city landmarks.

Taylor, Peter. *Summons to Memphis*. New York: Knopf Publishing Group, 1986. Celebrated and award-winning Tennessee writer Peter Taylor won the Pulitzer Prize for fiction for this novel in 1986. Phillip Carver returns home to Tennessee at the request of his three older sisters to talk his father out of remarrying. In so doing, he is forced to confront a troubling family history. This is a classic of American literature, set in a South that is fading away.

Wright, Richard. *Black Boy.* New York: Chelsea House, 2006. The 1945 memoir of African American writer Wright recounts several years of residency in Memphis. His portrayal of segregation and racism in Memphis and Mississippi are still powerful today.

FOOD

Lewis, Edna, and Scott Peacock. *The Gift of Southern Cooking: Recipes and Revelations from Two Great American Cooks.* New York: Knopf Publishing Group, 2003. Grande dame of Southern food Lewis and son-of-the-soil chef Peacock joined forces on this seminal text of Southern cuisine. It demystifies, documents, and inspires. Ideal for those who really care about Southern foodways.

Lundy, Ronnie, ed. *Cornbread Nation 3.* Chapel Hill: University of North Carolina Press, 2006. The third in a series of collections on Southern food and cooking. Published in collaboration with the Southern Foodways Alliance, which is dedicated to preserving and celebrating Southern food traditions, the Cornbread Nation collection is an ode to food traditions large and small. Topics include paw-paws, corn, and pork. *Cornbread Nation 2* focused on barbecue. *Cornbread Nation 1* was edited by restaurateur and Southern food celebrant John Egerton.

Internet and Digital Resources

TOURIST INFORMATION
Memphis Convention and Visitors Bureau
www.memphistravel.com
The official travel website for Memphis has listings of hotels, attractions, and events. You can also download coupons, request a visitors guide, or book hotels. The bureau also offers a free smartphone app called Memphis Travel Guide.

Tennessee Department of Tourism Development
www.tnvacation.com
On Tennessee's official tourism website you can request a visitors guide, search for upcoming events, or look up details about hundreds of attractions, hotels, and restaurants. This is a great resource for suggested scenic drives.

The Memphis Flyer

www.memphisflyer.com

Memphis's alternative weekly newspaper publishes entertainment listings and article archives on its website.

Memphis Magazine

www.memphismagazine.com

Good restaurant reviews and useful event listings. Subscriptions available online ($15 annually).

The Tennessean

www.tennessean.com

Nashville's major newspaper posts news, entertainment, sports, and business stories online. Sign up for a daily newsletter of headlines from Music City or search the archives.

PARKS AND RECREATION

Tennessee State Parks

www.state.tn.us/environment/parks

An online directory of all Tennessee state parks, this site provides useful details, including campground descriptions, cabin rental information, and the lowdown on activities.

TVA Lake Info

This free mobile app lists recreational dam release schedules for across the state.

HISTORY

Tennessee Civil War 150

A free mobile app provides quick-hit history lessons about Civil War battle sites, plus information about visiting them.

Tennessee Encyclopedia of History and Culture

www.tennesseeencyclopedia.net

The online edition of an excellent reference book, this website is a great starting point on all topics Tennessee. Articles about people, places, and events are written by hundreds of experts. Online entries are updated regularly.

INDEX

List of Maps

Photo Credits

Also Available

MAP SYMBOLS

▦▦▦ Expressway	★ Highlight	✗ Airfield	♪ Golf Course
▦▦▦ Primary Road	○ City/Town	✈ Airport	▣ Parking Area
▦▦▦ Secondary Road	◉ State Capital	▲ Mountain	▦ Archaeological Site
▪▪▪ Unpaved Road	◈ National Capital	✚ Unique Natural Feature	▌ Church
- - - Trail	★ Point of Interest		
⋯⋯ Ferry	• Accommodation	🀆 Waterfall	▊ Gas Station
~~ Railroad	▾ Restaurant/Bar	▲ Park	◌ Glacier
▦▦▦ Pedestrian Walkway	▪ Other Location	▯ Trailhead	▨ Mangrove
▥▥▥ Stairs	Λ Campground	✦ Skiing Area	▨ Reef
			▥ Swamp

CONVERSION TABLES

°C = (°F - 32) / 1.8
°F = (°C x 1.8) + 32
1 inch = 2.54 centimeters (cm)
1 foot = 0.304 meters (m)
1 yard = 0.914 meters
1 mile = 1.6093 kilometers (km)
1 km = 0.6214 miles
1 fathom = 1.8288 m
1 chain = 20.1168 m
1 furlong = 201.168 m
1 acre = 0.4047 hectares
1 sq km = 100 hectares
1 sq mile = 2.59 square km
1 ounce = 28.35 grams
1 pound = 0.4536 kilograms
1 short ton = 0.90718 metric ton
1 short ton = 2,000 pounds
1 long ton = 1.016 metric tons
1 long ton = 2,240 pounds
1 metric ton = 1,000 kilograms
1 quart = 0.94635 liters
1 US gallon = 3.7854 liters
1 Imperial gallon = 4.5459 liters
1 nautical mile = 1.852 km

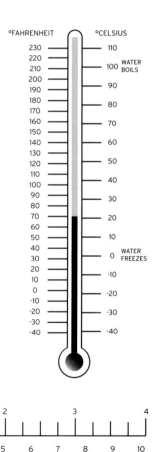

MOON MEMPHIS

Avalon Travel
an imprint of Perseus Books
a division of Hachette Book Group
1700 Fourth Street
Berkeley, CA 94710, USA
www.moon.com

Editor: Kimberly Ehart
Series Manager: Kathryn Ettinger
Copy Editor: Rosemarie Leenerts
Graphics and Production Coordinator: Lucie Ericksen
Cover Design: Faceout Studios, Charles Brock
Interior Design: Domini Dragoone
Moon Logo: Tim McGrath
Map Editor: Albert Angulo
Cartographers: Brian Shotwell and Karin Dahl
Indexer: Greg Jewett

ISBN-13: 978-1-63121-367-0
ISSN: 2472-0364

Printing History
1st Edition — August 2016
5 4 3 2 1